Welcome to your new home !

All the best.

Chris

TOTTERIDGE

A Buckinghamshire Village

A watercolour by Mary Giles, dated 1898, showing Totteridge Common, Totteridge House and Hicks Farm.

TOTTERIDGE

A Buckinghamshire Village

CHRIS GLADSTONE

Phillimore

2000

Published by
PHILLIMORE & CO. LTD.
Shopwyke Manor Barn, Chichester, West Sussex

ISBN 1 86077 157 2

Printed and bound in Great Britain by
THE CROMWELL PRESS
Trowbridge, Wiltshire

To Jan, for her patience

CONTENTS

LIST OF ILLUSTRATIONS ix

INTRODUCTION xi

LIST OF SUBSCRIBERS xiii

1. SUSPICIONS OF ANTIQUITY 1

2. MEDIEVAL MURK 6

3. INDUSTRIAL EXPANSION 14

4. THE 20TH CENTURY—FROM OPULENCE TO OBSCURITY 32

5. SITES OF SPECIAL INTEREST 60

BIBLIOGRAPHY 77

INDEX 79

LIST OF ILLUSTRATIONS

Frontispiece: Totteridge Common, Totteridge House and Hicks Farm, 1898

1. Bryant's map of 1824 2
2. Bassetsbury Manor House 11
3. Ordnance Survey map, 1832 18
4. White Cottage, *c.*1873-5 20
5. Farmland behind Bunces Farm, *c.*1870s 22
6. Auction notice relating to Bassetsbury Manor 23
7. Totteridge Common and House 24
8. A postcard of King's Wood 25
9. Totteridge Post Office 26-7
10. Ordnance Survey map, 1898 29
11. Cherry pickers in Totteridge 30
12. Totteridge Common, *c.*1910 31
13. Totteridge Lane looking towards Terriers, *c.*1909 33
14. Totteridge Lane, *c.*1913 34
15. Totteridge Hill, 1928 35
16. Ordnance Survey map, 1925 37
17. The opening of Terriers School, 1 July 1928 38
18. The view up Totteridge Hill, *c.*1930 40
19. The top of Totteridge Road, *c.*1930 41
20. Totteridge Lane below the *Dolphin*, 1935 42
21. Ordnance Survey map, 1938 43
22. Ernest Turner's Sports Club First XI Football team, 1951-2 44
23. The gallant men of Totteridge ARP 46
24. The children of Totteridge celebrating VE Day 47
25. The children of Totteridge and Terriers at
    Terriers School, May Day 1948 48
26. A painting of Hicks Farm by E. Leeder, early 1950s 49
27. The Coronation party for the children of The Crescent
    and the Drives, June 1953 50
28. Miss Elsie Carter, King's Wood County First School's
    first head teacher 51

29. Seven sets of twins attended King's Wood County First
       School in the 1950s.. 52
30. Pupils at King's Wood First School in the 1950s 53
31. Ordnance Survey map, 1950................................. 54
32. The original Woodman's Cottage, mid-1960s 56
33. St Andrews Mission Church, c.1904......................... 57
34. Sir Philip Rose by Spy, in *Vanity Fair*, 1881 62
35. Front of the auction notice for Totteridge House
       and Farm, 1910 64
36. Plan from the prospectus of Totteridge Farm Park, c.1911 65
37. Totteridge House today.................................... 67
38. Painting of John Byron and his ships *Dolphin* and *Tamar*........ 69
39. The *Dolphin*, c.1880s 70-1
40. Old Beams today.. 74

INTRODUCTION

I moved into High Wycombe in 1987 and then into Totteridge in 1994. At first, my impression of Totteridge was the same as that of most people of Wycombe: a developed section to the north of the main town which served as a convenient short-cut between the London and Amersham Roads. Indeed, the very name 'Totteridge' seemed to exist only on maps, for no signposts to the village are in evidence and the area is apparently defined solely by the confusing and scattered array of streets bearing the name (Totteridge Road, Lane, Avenue and Drive). Where, and what, was this Totteridge?

My curiosity was further fuelled when I started to wander through the area. I noticed a grand country house next to a common, an ancient beamed cottage hiding behind a dense hedge, an old pub with stables attached and unusual loops in the road, all flanked by the imposing King's Wood. This settlement clearly had a story to tell. I started in the most obvious place, High Wycombe Library, but was quickly dismayed at the shortage of information on offer. No details, but passing references only, were made to the area and even the local history societies in Wycombe could offer no further enlightenment. The only practical suggestion I received was 'Speak to the locals', and so that is exactly what I started to do.

Now, several years later, after speaking to numerous local inhabitants, many trips to various libraries, countless forays through the streets and woods, and maybe an excursion or two to the *Dolphin*, the fascinating story of Totteridge has finally emerged from the historical mist. It has proved to be a story worth telling and shows the settlement to have developed a clear character of its own, distinct from the bustling town of Wycombe in the valley far below. Totteridge has never made history but has always reflected it, and deserves to be recorded in its own right before it becomes irredeemably engulfed by that 20th-century blight, urban development.

Before proceeding, I would like to express my sincere thanks to everyone who has helped me in my quest. Special thanks are extended to David Gantzel, who has been an unending source of encouragement and fascinating archive material. I have been in contact with very many long-term inhabitants of Totteridge but would like to express my thanks in particular to Pam Ailward, Alec Chilton, David Cox, Tim Edmonds, Joan

Fane, Doug and Lorraine Hodson, Ernest Howes, Eddie Hoing, Marcel Leeder, Michael Montag, Brenda O'Brien, Brian and Doreen Pollard, Dennis Plumridge, Sylvia Scott, John Smith, Iris Soundy, Edith Turnock and John Veysey, all of whom have provided wonderful tales of Totteridge times past! There have also been a host of others who provided more information and who are too numerous to mention in person, and so a huge general 'thank you' to everyone!

In addition, my sincere thanks go to Martin Rickard of High Wycombe Library, who has kindly consented to the publication of many of the photographs used; to Dr. Eileen Scarff of St George's Chapel, Windsor, who has been most helpful in providing archive details of Bassetsbury Manor; and to the Buckinghamshire County Record Office and Chepping Wycombe Parish Council, both of whom were the willing source of more historical miscellanea.

During the pre-publication promotion, I received a great deal of help in publicising the book. My special thanks go to my daughter Rebecca and Lucy and Sarah Bowden who spent many hours on the door-to-door leafleting, and to the *Bucks Free Press* and *South Bucks Leader* for their assistance. My thanks are also extended to businesses and local public centres which very kindly agreed to site more leaflets, and these included the Wycombe Museum, High Wycombe Library, High Wycombe Tourist Information, the *Dolphin* public house, the *Golden Fleece* public house, Ajantha's (Totteridge Stores), St Wulfstan's Catholic Church, Highworth Combined School, King's Wood Infant School, King's Wood Junior School, St Francis of Assisi of Terriers and Totteridge, Totteridge and District Social Club, Hatters Lane School, St Andrew's Church, Terriers Post Office, Hazlemere Library and the Cottage Bookshop (Penn).

At this juncture, it is wise to mention that much of the information relating to the 20th-century has been passed to me by word of mouth and, even though I have transcribed the details as accurately as possible, certain errors are bound to have slipped in, for which I apologise in advance. I also acknowledge the fact that other fascinating stories of Totteridge may exist that I have not yet been able to unearth. Even so, I hope that the story that unfolds will provide an enjoyable and entrancing portrait of a small village, once flourishing but now tottering on the verge of obscurity.

LIST OF SUBSCRIBERS

Pita J. Abbott
Mrs. Pamela J. Ailward (née Howes)
William Albert Aldridge 1917-72
Mrs. E. Allnutt
Susan Lynn Attwood
The Banks Family
Belinda Barton
Christine M. Bealer
Jim and Brenda Beckford
K. and R. Benson
John S. Bignell
Mr. and Mrs. D.W. Blackman
John F. Blandford
Noel and Janet Bobbin
D.W. and C.M. Bosanco-Mitchell
The Bowden Family
Derek Bradshaw
Graham Bradshaw
Mike Bridgefoot
Ian R. Briscoe
Dr. and Mrs J. Brockless
Mrs. Beric Browne
Patricia Wendy Burch
Mrs. Christine Caine (née Lawrence)
Peter, June and Martin Campbell
D.G. and P.A. Carr
Paul Chambers and Anna Chambers (née Symonds)
Chris, Juliet, Ian, and Jessica Chandler
Mr. and Mrs. A.K. Church
David C. Church
David J. Church
Tony, Michael and Mary Clarke
P.Y. Correy
Mr. and Mrs. C.R. Crofton
The Cronk Family
Mrs. Gillian Curran and Family
Beryl Dafter
Bobby Dafter
Chris, Richard and Dominic Davis-Foster
Daphne Deegan
Mr. and Mrs. G. Desimone
Dave Dixon
Rodney K. Doel
Colin Donald
Mr. G. Dormer

Joan Downes
David Dyson
Mr. B.P. Ebrey and Miss Z.A. Davies
Alan Eckford
Tim Edmonds
John L.G. Felix
The Fell Family
Raymond Finch
Jean Finlan (Teacher)
Mr. B.J. Fletcher
David Flinders
Ian and Daphne Ford
The Francis Family
David H. Gantzel
David and Kathy Gatrell
Mrs. Brenda Gillson
Andy Gladstone
Mrs. Ann Gladstone
Philip P. Grapes
A.R. and D.M. Green
Miles Green
Geoff and Pamela Haines
Mrs. Gwen Hall (née Stretton)
Teresa Hancock
Stuart and Patricia Harley
Julie S. Harris
W.L. Harris
Eric and Millicent Harvey
The Hatters Lane School
Ellen Hawes
Jennifer Hawkins
Mrs. K.M. Hearfield
Ray Hedinburgh
Mrs. M.M.C. Holder
G. Holroyd
Ian S. Horwood
Frederick Michael Gladstone Houghton
Mr. and Mrs. M. Howarth
Samantha Howden and Daniel Kaljura
Mr. Barry Howes
Ernest Howes
Mike and Pam Howlett
Alan Hunt
Mrs. I. Hunt
Stephen Hunt
Jaswinder Jhalli

Mary Jones (née Smith)
Valerie Jones
Catherine Keating
Roy Keegan
Christopher T. Kenney
Kingswood Junior School
The Kipping Family
Eileen Kipping (née Phillips)
Martin Kipping
Alan and Sue Kitchen and Family
A.H. Lavers
Marcel Leeder
Micheal Lines
Emily Long
P.J. Lowe
David Loxley
Irene L. Lucock
Josephine Martin
Christopher Edward Matthews
Ernest P. Maunder
Mills Family
Group Captain Roy Morris
Jacqui May Morrison
Peter and Carol Mortlock
Peter Mulville
Mr. David Murray
Michael Terry Newell
Karen and David Newton (née Brayley)
Janet Nicholl
Mr. Obren and Deyan Simic
Brenda O'Brien—Highworth School
Mr. and Mrs. T. Oxlade
The Page Family
Olive Mary Parkin
Graham Paterson
Henry Terry Pattinson
Lorraine Carol Pepper-McCrudden
Diane Phillips
Andrew Pickup
David Pickup
Jonathan Pickup
Mr. and Mrs. G. Pierce
Julie, Martin and Hazel Plummer
Brian and Doreen Pollard
Elizabeth Porter
B. Puddephatt
Mr. and Mrs. Raja
Cyril George Rance
A. Ridgley
Margaret and Dennis Ridgley
Anthony M. Robinson
Barbara Russell
Pam Sanger-Walker
Andy, Jan, Ben and Sam Saunders
Colin J. Seabright

Martin Shepherd
Michael Jon Silverthorne
Mr. and Mrs. R.F. Simmons
Brian W. Simpson
Pamela Skeels (née Holder)
Diane Smith
Mrs. P. Smith
Susanne Smith
John Smithson
Mrs. Iris B. Soundy
Mr. Barry Spicer
James Stacey
Joan Stacey
Annette and Alex Steel
Bill and Hilary Stephenson
Julian Stevens
Matthew Stevens
Peter and Erica Stevens
Eddie and Gill Strevens
D. and J. Styles
Pam and Cliff Styles
Mr. and Mrs. C.M. Swallow
Ruth Talmer (née Archer)
Mr. and Mrs. A.L. Taylor
Patricia Ann Taylor
Peggy Taylor
Joan M. Tennant
Mrs. C. Thompson
Win Tilbury
Elizabeth Tucker
Janice Tucker
Richard J. Turner
Edith and Ron Turnock
Mrs. Betty Underwood (née Stretton)
The Walker Family
Adrian and Jackie Walker
John and Sheila Ward
Martin Ward
Simon Ward
Mr. and Mrs. Rodney Watts
Paul Webb
Valerie and Dudley Weeks
Mrs. Joyce Westwood
Mrs. J.M.C. White
Miss K.J. White
Ian Whitelock
Malcolm Wiles
Mrs. Gill Wilkinson
C. and D. Williams
Angus Williamson
Phil Williams
Kay Willis
David Winterburn
Linda Wright
Bill and Phyllis Young

One

SUSPICIONS OF ANTIQUITY

The tale of Totteridge begins many centuries ago. The first historical record of the name dates to the late 12th century but, like many other settlements in the area, its true origins go back a great deal further. It is an unfortunate fact, however, that the majority of settlements in England lack any historical reference prior to Domesday. The only tool for delving into the early evolution of such places is often archaeological research, and this by its very nature can usually provide only scraps of information and a limited image of man's overall impact on the landscape. In the case of Totteridge, however, not even archaeology can help us look into the past, for no definite pre-medieval structures or artefacts have yet come to light. This may not necessarily be because there is nothing there to find, but is more likely the result of lack of research in the area. The darkest origins of Totteridge must be sought elsewhere.

The first clue is the name 'Totteridge' itself. The official meaning is 'Tota's Ridge' or 'look-out hill', from the Old English 'tot' (look-out place) or 'tot aern' (look-out house), and 'hrycg' (ridge). The place-name offers two possible explanations. The first is that it does indeed mean 'the ridge of Tota', and there is historical evidence that might support this theory. In Domesday Book of 1086, there is frequent reference to Azor, son of Toti, who held much land, especially towards the northern end of Buckinghamshire. Earlier than this, it is recorded that a prominent Dane called Toti (presumably Azor's father) owned much land in the Buckinghamshire and Oxfordshire areas in the early half of the 11th century. There is a possibility that Totteridge was owned and named after this man (or perhaps a namesake), evolving over time from Toti's to Tota's Ridge.

The second possible explanation relates to the 'look-out hill'. The study of place-names demonstrates numerous examples of settlements named after topographical features, often in conjunction with personal names, and it has been suggested that some of these names may have originated from the Iron Age or even earlier times. It is also accepted in place-name studies that the compound 'tot-earn' can be a reliable guide to the existence of an Iron-Age hillfort, although 'tot' on its own could mean no more than a look-out point. The root of 'Totteridge' is uncertain,

1   Bryant's map of 1824 showing Totteridge Castle.

however, and so this place-name evidence connecting it with the Iron Age
must be treated with caution.

Another tantalising clue to the prehistory of Totteridge emerges in the
shape of Totteridge Castle, the only firm evidence of which is provided by
a reference on a map by Bryant dated to 1824. The map was produced at
a time when Totteridge was a small village consisting of a scatter of houses
and farms and, although somewhat indistinct, the map does name several of
the larger local landmarks, including the *Dolphin* public house and Totteridge
Castle, the latter apparently sited at the north end of the settlement. The
only published research conducted into the castle was in 1931 by Francis
Colmer, who wrote an article in the *Bucks Free Press*, and his conclusions are
of great interest. Colmer began his search by asking the local residents what
they knew of this castle but he largely drew a blank. He approached an
elderly man in the *Dolphin* and was told, 'There bain't never been no car'sle
here. I'm in my seventy-five, and I'd ha' seed un if so be it had.' Similar
inquiries recently produced similar, if not so lyrical, responses! Colmer
continued in his quest and, drawing on the place-name evidence, concluded
that the pre-Roman 'aboriginal folk of Totteridge' inhabited the north-west
corner of King's Wood among a large earthworked enclosure that ran from

the approximate site of the *Dolphin* north across the top of the wood. However, no physical evidence for a substantial enclosure of this variety now remains, the earthworks that Colmer witnessed probably being linear field or territory boundaries behind the Tyzack Road development of, most likely, a medieval date (see Chapter 2).

Bryant's map implies that Totteridge Castle is located on a spur of land approximately where Highworth Combined School now stands. The original loop in Totteridge Lane here is greatly exaggerated, which helps to locate it more precisely. The earliest map of Totteridge that shows buildings dates to 1774 and a structure does appear on the site of the school. This building at the time may have been named Little Totteridge House (from an 1870s map), or may have been Totteridge Castle. It is definitely true, if unfortunate, there was never a genuine medieval castle here, for the historical and archaeological evidence would be unmistakable. Could the building have been a grand country house that the owner in his vanity called a Castle? The only other possibility is that a major feature known locally as a 'castle' did in fact exist, under or close to the house.

The term 'castle' is often used to describe Iron-Age hillforts, a local example being Desborough Castle, traditionally classed as Iron-Age although recent excavation has pointed towards a medieval origin. Evidence of prolific settlement in this period abounds in the fertile Wye valley and, although no firm archaeological evidence has yet appeared on the northern ridge above the valley, it is reasonable to suppose that the area saw some activity. The site of Totteridge Castle, on raised ground controlling the upper end of the ridge, would be ideally suited to strategic settlement. Further suggestive of an early important settlement on the site is the positioning of the original track up the ridge, holding a primarily straight course up the ridge from the Wye valley before curving deliberately towards the Castle and then veering sharply right to hug the border of the semi-circular boundary before straightening once again towards Terriers. This landscape configuration can most clearly be seen on a map dated to 1925 (fig.16). It is tempting to conclude that this semi-circle describes the remaining half of an Iron-Age settlement, the other half of which has long since been developed away. If this is indeed the case, the full diameter of the earthwork would have been approximately 150m., larger than Desborough Castle. Other possible local prehistoric earthworks include the south end of King's Wood overlooking the Micklefield valley, containing bank-and-ditch earthworks of an Iron-Age character, and, in Totteridge itself, an earthwork bank, almost directly below the site on the edge of King's Wood, and a distinctive ridge bisecting the field from Totteridge to Terriers. As for the elusive 'castle' itself, no visible traces now remain, long since buried under generations of development on the site.

Throughout the centuries Wycombe has had its share of military activity. During the civil war in the reign of King Stephen (1135-54), the motte on Castle Hill was besieged and it is known that temporary earthwork camps were constructed in areas of high activity at this time. During the 17th-century Civil War, the Thames valley was the centre of the conflict in the early years, with Wycombe being a Parliamentarian stronghold. There was a battle on the Rye in 1642 and in the following year Wycombe was heavily raided by Royalist forces following the Battle of Chalgrove. The 'castle' at Totteridge may have had its origin during such engagements (or have been reoccupied), although the place-name evidence suggests a more ancient ancestry.

The link with the Iron Age is, however, only speculative and relies purely on circumstantial evidence. But given our knowledge of other Iron-Age features in the Wycombe area, it is almost certain there was activity in this period on the north side of the Wye valley, although whether Totteridge Castle is a genuine part of the Iron-Age landscape remains a question that only future archaeological research can answer.

History gives visibility to Totteridge only from the 12th century onwards. Before this time, a certain amount of hypothesis must be used to reconstruct life in the area. Archaeological evidence has shown that the Wycombe region has been occupied almost continually since at least Bronze-Age times, with the most intensive settlement naturally concentrated along the fertile Wye valley. Prehistoric artefacts have been discovered in the area over the years, notably a Neolithic/Bronze-Age flint arrowhead at Terriers and a Bronze-Age palstave axe at Hazlemere, although the relative paucity of finds suggests there was no substantial settlement in the vicinity at this time.

As mentioned above, there is substantial evidence of Iron-Age activity in the area and, following on from this, the Roman villa on the Rye gives us a clear indication of the area's agricultural prosperity. The nearest villa neighbour to Wycombe yet found is at Amersham and it is highly probable that the present A404 Amersham Road traces the route of an ancient track between these two important settlements, dating possibly to pre-Roman times. The track passes close to Totteridge and through Hazlemere, where both Roman and Saxon artefacts have been recovered. In 1929, at the construction site of the Green Hill Estate at Terriers, on the brow of the hill overlooking the Hughenden valley, was discovered the remains of a building believed at the time to be either late Iron-Age or early Roman. In addition, there is evidence of Roman settlement close by at Hazlemere, where a variety of artefacts unearthed close to the Hazlemere turnpike area in 1826 indicated the possibility of a Roman burial ground or farmstead.

Saxons are known to have inhabited Hazlemere and the Widmer End area, where hunting lodges belonging to several of their kings existed and where several Saxon finds have been discovered, notably an inhumation whose subject possessed five gold chains and pendants. There is a strong possibility that more evidence of ancient settlements from all periods may yet come to light along the route from Wycombe to Amersham. To the north-east of Terriers lie the remains of the deserted medieval hamlet of Pirenore (possibly called Iminge Canonicorum – '*the innings or intake of the monks*'), which is suspected to have early origins as its name is Saxon for 'the hill where the pear trees grow', although no solid evidence for Saxon occupation has yet been found. From the earliest historical records onwards, Totteridge had been settled and farmed, doubtless contributing towards the growth and prosperity of the town of Wycombe itself. The early evolution of the settlement is obscure and it is only from A.D. 1179 that the village emerges as an independent development with a character markedly distinct from that of Wycombe below.

Two

MEDIEVAL MURK

A.D. 1179. Christendom was in turmoil. Most of Europe's military might was crusading in the Holy Land against the Muslims under the formidable Saladin. The slaughter and bloodshed in this land of heat and dust was appalling, as both sides, fighting fanatically in the name of religious right, continued to battle relentlessly by sword and axe. Two years previously, the Crusaders, led by Baldwin IV, had narrowly prevented Jerusalem from falling as they struggled for survival in this alien territory. In England, King Henry II was on the throne as the country lay in the grip of radical social change. A few years earlier, in 1170, Thomas Becket had been openly murdered in Canterbury Cathedral and the same year saw widespread insurrection by the powerful barons against Henry. The insurrection was quickly suppressed and Henry introduced a series of measures to limit severely the power of the barons and install a more formal system of justice.

Little is known about how this national and international discord affected the inhabitants of the Wye valley. The first real glimpse of life in the area comes from the 1086 Domesday survey of land ownership, commissioned by the new Norman King William. Totteridge was not mentioned, being only a small and insignificant agricultural settlement, whilst 'Wicube' itself was recorded as the second most populous manor in Buckinghamshire, with a thriving economy based around the numerous mills along the river. The survey does mention the woodland of Wycombe, large enough for 500 pigs, and King's Wood may have formed a part of this area. Another large Domesday settlement was at Amersham, which was occupied continuously from at least Roman times, strongly suggesting continuity of use of the Wycombe–Amersham lane.

In the 1160s, Wycombe was owned by the Crown, who bestowed a life grant of the manor on the baron Thomas Basset in 1171. In 1179, Thomas was succeeded by Gilbert Basset and it is in these early manorial documents that Totteridge is first mentioned as a part of the manorial territory. Wycombe was divided into several small estates along the length of the Wye valley and one of these estates was called Gynant's Fee, in the care of the Crown and situated on the north side of the valley, reaching up possibly as far as Totteridge. On his death in 1189, Henry II was succeeded by his first son

Richard who, in his turn, died in 1199, and was succeeded by his brother John. Richard had spent the first four years of his reign out of England in the Holy Land, leaving the country without a ruler, and the domestic taxes imposed to fund his zealous crusading activities had crippled the economy. When John became king, money was needed quickly and one option he pursued was to sell grants of manors. On 10 June 1203, the Manor of Wycombe was split and permanent grants sold to the barons Alan Basset (a kinsman of Gilbert) and Ralph Vipont. Basset had the lion's share of Wycombe, including Totteridge, and his estate thereafter became known as Bassetsbury Manor.

Totteridge has been intricately bound up with the fortunes of Bassetsbury Manor until relatively recent times, but from the 13th through to the 18th centuries only scant records exist relating to the village itself. The development of the settlement seems to have been obscured by both the larger concerns of the Manor and also the general historical murk of the medieval period. An impression of the evolution of Totteridge through these ages can therefore be gained largely by examining the fate of Bassetsbury Manor.

In the 13th century, Chepping Wycombe, as it was known, was only a small settlement in the valley bottom surrounded by fertile farmland that stretched up the valley sides, probably little changed since Roman times. Basset and Vipont were powerful barons who were both present at the signing of the Magna Carta later in 1215, and who seemed to know how to run their estates profitably. In the 13th century, the Archdeaconry of Buckinghamshire was within the See of Lincoln and the See struggled fervently for several centuries in its battle to stamp out heresy, for which the south of the county was notorious. At this time as well, the Crown was demanding all manner of foodstuffs from the home counties and, as a result, the corn mills along the Wye flourished as they shipped wheat constantly down the Thames to London. Bassetsbury Manor was booming and the farmland of Totteridge no doubt contributed to its economic wealth.

Alan Basset died in 1231, succeeded by his son Gilbert, and in 1271 the Manor passed to the Despenser family by marriage. The Despensers were favourites of Edward II and became his advisers, but this celebrated existence was not destined to last long. The Despenser family lost favour and in 1321 their political opponents devastated all their manors, including Bassetsbury. The family managed to hold onto the Manor until 1326 when Hugh le Despenser was executed for high treason and the Manor reverted to the Crown. Bassetsbury then passed through various hands until it eventually became a part of the Duchy of Lancaster when Mary, wife of Henry (later Duke of Lancaster and King Henry IV), succeeded to the Manor in 1373.

The 14th century saw very turbulent times. England endured the Hundred Years War against France and the Scottish War of Independence,

King Edward II was deposed and murdered, private armies were roaming the land, the Church was being reformed, and the peasants revolted in 1377. Buckinghamshire was not actively involved in the Peasants Revolt, which was centred mainly on eastern and south-eastern England, although the widespread insurrection in the home counties must have caused dramatic disruption to all agricultural communities close to London. On the positive side, the early 14th century saw the rise of craftsmen and merchants within towns throughout England and a new class of tenant farmers arose as feudalism finally died out following the decline of baronial power.

The next historical reference to Totteridge, albeit an indirect and tentative one, dates from the mid-14th century. The First Wycombe Ledger Book contains the following record, dated 11 March 1354:

> Memorandum: that at that great Gild held on Tuesday next before the feast of St Gregory in the twenty-eighth year of the reign of King Edward III, the mayor and community granted to John Lokyer a certain curtilage situated in the fee of the Abbess of Godstow; and it lies between the tenement once Richard Toterugge's on the western side, and the tenement once Thomas Gilbard's on the eastern side: which curtilage Alan att Wythge bequeathed by his will to the wardens for the time being of the lights of the blessed Mary: to have and to hold to the aforesaid John Lokyer and his heirs of the chief lords of that fee for the service due therefrom, and for the customary 4s.; paying therefor 12d. annually to the wardens of the church for all services.

At this time in the medieval period, surnames had become firmly established, often derived from family associations, nick-names, occupations or place-names. The record above unfortunately sheds no light on the village of Totteridge itself and can serve only to suggest that Richard Toterugge may have come from the village and owned land in other parts of the Wycombe area.

Totteridge continued to keep its historical head low during the 15th century. It is known that in the early part of the century, Thomas Hampden had purchased lands called Toterugge from William Clarke of Wycombe. Thomas came from an ancient and wealthy Buckinghamshire family of landowners, his son John eventually becoming Mayor of Wycombe in 1449. Before this, however, Totteridge had already passed from the Hampden to the Cotyngham family, who were also notable personages of the time, Robert Cotyngham being installed as Mayor in 1445. The shortage of historical references at this time is not uncommon for a small agricultural settlement that was probably made up of only two or three farms, and we can assume that the community laboured away much as it had done for generations, contributing to the economic life of the Manor and, more generally, to the growing prosperity of Chepping Wycombe.

We do know that the general area did have a certain prominence at this time, for a small hamlet by the name of Pirenore occupied the fields to the north, close to Grange Farm, between the present Terriers and Widmer End settlements. Pirenore is believed to have existed from at least Norman times, and possibly even Saxon, and emerges historically in 1159, when it was inhabited by a community of monks from Missenden Abbey; it was mysteriously abandoned sometime in the Middle Ages. South of this hamlet and running parallel to the current Amersham Road lay the path known as Ladies Mile that is believed to have been a drover's track leading from Hazlemere to Wycombe market. In addition, close to Pirenore at Four Ashes also lie the buried remains of a building reputed to be the castle of Simon de Montfort, a very prominent political figure in England in the mid-13th century, although the structure is more likely to be a country residence or hunting lodge built by his descendants. There appears to have been a great deal of activity in this area at this time, which would undoubtedly have affected the adjacent village of Totteridge.

The first cracks in the economic stability of Bassetsbury Manor started to appear in the 15th century. The Manor had been thriving for two centuries, but at the end of the medieval period, which brought radical change to the fabric of society, with Chepping Wycombe expanding on the back of the new class of tradesman, Bassetsbury began its slow decline. Although the Manor could still be regarded as prosperous, some parts of it, like land in Totteridge, was sold off. The Manor remained within the Duchy of Lancaster throughout the reign of Henry IV, who died in 1422, and the Wars of the Roses between the Houses of Lancaster and York from 1450-71. In 1483 the Manor was granted to the Dean and Canons of St George's Chapel, Windsor, by whom it was held for the next 400 years.

Totteridge finally starts to emerge from its long obscurity in the 16th century as the records relating to the area become more common. The ancient trackway across the ridge that we now know as Totteridge Lane is first mentioned in some deeds dated to 1517, in the reign of Henry VIII:

> William Aley of Wycombe and Edmund Mason of Stokenchurch grant to Richard Reynolds five acres and one half-acre of arable land and one acre of woodland in the fields of Wycombe: of which three acres of arable and the wood are in hyfield (High Field): the arable lying between land belonging to Robert Shereborn, Bishop (Sc. of Chichester) once Stokton's, on the east, and the land of Robert Astbroke's on the west; these three acres run lengthwise from a lane called Totrygelane on the north to lands belonging to Robert Astbroke and John Mundy on the south.

This document is the first mention of High Field, an area on the Hicks Farm side of Totteridge, its name remembered in Highfield Wood, which largely disappeared during the 19th century. As the medieval manorial lands began to split up, the entrepreneurs moved in and the prime farm land in the Wycombe area, including Totteridge as above, became highly prized. The settlement may well have continued to grow and thrive purely on this agricultural foundation for the next few centuries. The catalyst that turned Totteridge from a collection of farms into a desirable and prosperous village was not the farmland on its own, however, but the economic gold-mine that lay in its back pocket—King's Wood.

The origin of King's Wood and its name are lost in time. The name could refer to the Saxon kings who hunted at Hazlemere and also possibly in King's Wood, although it is more likely that it was named after King John who used it as a part of his hunting grounds after he had issued the grant of Bassetsbury Manor in 1203. There is no doubt that the wood is of very ancient origin and could be one of the last surviving original parts of the Chiltern woodland unchanged over millennia. The earliest records relating to King's Wood show that it was a valuable economic asset that was extensively worked and managed as a part of the Bassetsbury estate. Despite selling off much of the land in Totteridge by the 16th century, the Manor retained possession of the wood until the late 19th century, providing it with regular income, as this 1541 record illustrates:

> Sale by Henry Wyllyams Clerk, one of the Canons of the King's free Chapel of St George, Windsor, and Steward of the same, to John Wellys of Chepyng Wycombe, baker, of ten hundred beche trees of the best and biggest in a wood or grove called Kynges woode in Chepyng Wycomb, and also of five Okes in the same Wood or in any other place within the lordship of the said College called Bassettysbury, for twenty-five pounds. Signed per me Henricum Williams. 26 September 1541.

Two more records dating to 1562 also serve to illustrate the importance of the wood in the affairs of the local community:

> 27 June 1562. Release by John Raunce of Bassetsbury in the parish of Chippinge Wycombe in the county of Bucks Gent. and Robert Raunce his son to the Dean and Canons of Kingswood reaching from Totrydge Grene to Sextens Corner,

and:

> Evidence of Ancient Men about the plot of wood adjoining King's wood in the parish of Cheping Wicombe in 1562. Richard Frympton of Penne, Bucks 60 years of age, William Ouldhowse of Penne 67, Nycholas Smewey 80, Thomas Grove 62 and 16 more. It hath been all our lives time and before as we have heard our parents say to be the master's of the queen's free Chapel of Windsor, and we never heard that the lord of Saint Johns Jerusalem that was or late nor any other had any plot there; with the marks and seals of nine.

2 Bassetsbury Manor House in the 1920s, pre-restoration, displaying several architectural features dating to the late Middle Ages.

Such territory disputes were commonplace and as a result clear boundaries would have been defined. Some of the low banks that can still be seen today on the more level areas of the wood may be evidence of these medieval territory markers, although many may also be a result of demarcating areas of woodland set aside for coppicing, the banks built to prevent livestock grazing on the young shoots. Coppicing would have been a vital requirement for the chair-making industry as it developed in Wycombe from the 18th century onwards and may have been a practice that had existed for many centuries previously. The Coppice Pond in the north-west of King's Wood may recall this activity in its name.

Several records dating from the 16th century provide us with a glimpse of life in Totteridge. Little Totteridge Farm was held by Andrew Deane in 1547 and consisted of 126 acres of land, which no doubt covered much of the later Terriers. In 1571, Robert Raunce, the lessee of Bassetsbury Manor, sub-let in Totteridge one messuage and two virgates of land to Isabella Forde of Bradenham, the fields variously known as Peasecroft, Barnefield, Hanging Grove, Long and Round Morrell (adjoining Highfield Wood, which formerly extended south of King's Wood across land belonging to Hicks Farm) and Haydell Croft. Another record dating to 1584 shows that Constantine Slater was the tenant of both King's Wood House and Kingsmead Farm down in the valley, as well as most of the farmland from King's Wood to the Rye, including Bowerdean. As King's Wood House was mentioned as being close to Totteridge Common, it is possible that it stood on the site of the later Totteridge House. Slater was fined 10s. as he had not repaired the gate 'that standeth at ye lane end (Wycombefield Lane) next into Totteridge, which gate is decayed to the great damage of the inhabitants thereaboute'. It is possible that Wycombefield Lane is the present Totteridge Road.

The fertility of the farmland and the increasing exploitation of the wood attracted more settlers to the area. The house known today as Old Beams had its origins in the latter half of the 16th-century, and two of the former farms in Totteridge, Hicks and Highfield, are reputed to have been essentially Elizabethan in style although an earlier origin is very probable. Indeed, until its destruction in the 1950s, Highfield Farm possessed an impressive knot-garden very reminiscent of Elizabethan times. There is also evidence that cock-fighting was once a pastime enjoyed in Totteridge, as a cockspur of Tudor style was recently discovered on Totteridge Green.

England was beginning to settle into the land we know today. The 16th century had seen the Dissolution of the Monasteries, war against France and the accession of Elizabeth I to the throne, followed by a period of rapid commercial development that brought prosperity to the nation. The military threat from Spain, arising from deep-rooted religious differences, culminated in the rout of the Armada in 1588, helping England to establish its position as the dominant power in the world.

After Elizabeth died in 1603, the Stuart dynasty began under James I, and troubled times lay ahead. Political squabbles and the mismanagement of foreign policy fuelled growing unrest in the corridors of power, finally erupting with the Civil War of 1642-9. This period of history was catastrophic for the town of Chepping Wycombe. The Thames Valley was the centre of conflict in the early years of the war, the King's forces based in Oxford and the Parliamentarian strength scattered around the home counties and the Midlands. Wycombe was firmly Parliamentarian and saw its first action in 1642 when a battle took place on the Rye at which over 1,200 men were reported to have been killed. Most of the Parliamentarian resistance in the area was concentrated in the Chiltern hills where the topography provided clear strategic advantages. John Hampden, a Buckinghamshire man, became one of the leading architects of the resistance to the Crown before the outbreak of the war and raised and commanded a regiment of foot, the Buckinghamshire Greencoats. In June 1643, he stopped the Royalist forces under Prince Rupert at Chalgrove as they marched towards Wycombe and Hampden himself was mortally wounded, dying at Thame several days later. One week after Chalgrove, the Royalists under Colonel Urry raided Wycombe and plundered the town.

The end of the war saw life in the agricultural communities around England slowly begin to settle back into familiar patterns. In the early part of the 17th century, King's Wood was leased by St George's Chapel to Sir Robert Johnson, at an annual rent of £45, although it is reported that in 1666 locals living in the vicinity of the wood had the right to cut fuel there. The farms of Totteridge continued to support the economy of Wycombe so that, by the time the industrial era was born in the 18th century, the community was strong and independent enough to take full advantage of the increased prosperity that the new age offered.

Three

INDUSTRIAL EXPANSION

Bassetsbury Manor had been steadily declining since the 15th century although as the 18th century opened it still represented a substantial force in the economic life of Wycombe. The earliest full survey of the Manor dates to *c.*1780 and reveals that its assets included a great deal of land along the Wye valley between the town and Pinions, some land at King's Mead, three mills (Loudwater Mill, Hedge Paper Mill and Bridge Mill), Oakridge Farm and King's Wood, which together portrays a varied and thriving economy. It is not known exactly when the village of Totteridge became independent of the Manor but it appears to have been one of the early casualties of the late-medieval belt-tightening, as the records of land sale in the previous chapter suggest. In 1717 the lease of the Manor was acquired by the Dashwood family although the Manor itself was still owned by the Dean and Canons of St George's Chapel, Windsor.

There are no records relating to Totteridge in the first half of the 18th century but we must assume that the agricultural life continued as normal. As the century progressed, the new Industrial Age was starting to change the fabric of life throughout Britain, offering wonderful opportunities to those willing to incorporate the developing technology into their existing businesses. The tollhouse at Terriers, situated on the main Hatfield–Reading toll road, was built in the mid-18th century and this increased accessibility would have attracted more trade to the area. The owners of Bassetsbury Manor understood that King's Wood was a valuable asset that could be worked even more efficiently and prosperously with the new machinery, as well as being transported more efficiently on the new roads. No direct evidence of this exists, but the growth and emergence of Totteridge as a thriving village by the end of the century suggests that the area had started to exploit its substantial economic potential, founded on both the farmland and wood. The Wycombe paper-making industry developed rapidly in the latter half of the 18th century and at the same time chair-making started to take off as well. The value of King's Wood was clear. A public house has been situated in the centre of the village since at least 1755 (see Chapter 5), its position next to the wood suggesting a steady trade serving both the agricultural community and the growing number of woodland labourers coming into the area.

A sorry tale relating to King's Wood originates from this time. In 1751, it is reported that a man named Thomas Grove accepted a bet of a gallon of beer that he could not run up one of the steepest parts of King's Wood. Thomas, whom we imagine to have been a little overweight, actually succeeded in this task, but when he reached the top, he unfortunately 'expired'. The hill was consequently named Breakheart Hill, as it has been known from that day forward.

In the early 1770s, the first large-scale maps of Britain began to appear, giving us our first real images of land previously hidden from history. The village of Totteridge finally comes to light and is shown to have been a settlement roughly scattered along the track known today as Totteridge Lane, as can be more clearly seen in a slightly later map dating to 1796. Definite structures are in evidence and can be identified as the farms that continued to exist until the mid-20th century (Hicks Farm, Totteridge Farm, Highfield Farm, Little Totteridge Farm at Terriers and Hatters Farm down Hatters Lane), Totteridge House itself, the *Dolphin* public house, the cottages now known as Old Beams, a building on the site of Highworth Combined School, and structures (probably houses) in the dip in the lane just below the *Dolphin*. In other words, Totteridge had all the elements of a small, primarily agricultural, community. The origin of most of these buildings remains in doubt, although it is likely that the farms (with the exception of Totteridge House Farm) had already existed for several centuries. The architectural style of both Highfield and Hicks Farms is believed to have dated back to at least Elizabethan times. It is also known that John Birch, who was elected burgess, Alderman and Mayor of Wycombe in 1769, was a farmer in Totteridge.

Totteridge was linked to Wycombe by two routes: the main road which still runs from Wycombe to Amersham, and the more minor track that has since developed into Totteridge Road. The latter route formed the main highway from Wycombe to Penn, winding its way up Totteridge Hill, past Hicks Farm, along the edge of Totteridge Common, and through King's Wood until it reached Tylers Green, and then to Penn.

As the 18th century closed, Chepping Wycombe was beginning to flourish as a town. Local resources were being exploited as extensively as possible and the economy was booming. The strength of the town derived from the Chiltern beechwoods and the industries dependent on them, and the long-term prosperity of the area seemed almost guaranteed. The land in the Wye valley itself had been farmed for centuries and was devoid of woodland, and so the paper and furniture industrialists of Wycombe scoured the south Buckinghamshire countryside in search of extensive and sustainable beechwoods to feed the growing market. King's Wood was an obvious and very handy source, although the majority of its crop must have fed

Bassetsbury Manor's own mills directly. The records of the Manor in the early 19th century show that the profitable management of the wood was a high priority given its dwindling fortunes, and in April 1805 the first detailed survey of the wood appears. Mr. Trumper, the surveyor, makes his report thus:

> The woods seem to be under better management at this time than they have hitherto been, but are now in a very poor state having been cut too hard and not a sufficient quantity of beech left to grow to a proper size so as to make the woods of any greater value, but it appears to me that King's Wood being a commonable wood and the cattle lying so very hard upon it the stock of beech is getting thin and it will be a difficulty to manage it so as to keep up its present value, unless it is managed with very great attention; the present bailiff Mr Lacey seems to pay every attention to the preservation of the young stock of oak and ash timber, and if properly attended to it will improve very fast there being a considerable quantity of young stores in King's Wood.

This report suggests that King's Wood had already been rigorously farmed for several decades or longer and was showing worrying signs of over-exploitation. It is also reported that it 'lies as a common wood' and, although always owned by Bassetsbury Manor, commoners had always enjoyed a number of privileges, including the limited extraction of raw materials such as clay, chalk and sand, and the grazing of livestock. To help monitor the various activities within the wood, Bassetsbury employed a wood bailiff and owned 'a small house and plot of ground joining to King's Wood in possession of the person who looks after King's Wood'. In 1800, it is also reputed that the wood was used as an exercise and training ground for the Military College, which was then based in Wycombe, in preparation to combat the forces of Napoleon in Europe. At this time, the wood and, by association, Totteridge, must have been a hive of activity.

Further surveys of Bassetsbury Manor have survived dating from the early 19th century. In 1813 the Manor House itself is reported to have been used primarily for general agricultural use, with two rooms converted into a single schoolroom for the 163 boys of the Royal Grammar School, whose own school was suffering building delays due to a temporary shortage of funds. The 1826 survey of the manor probably gives us the most vivid impression of its declining health. Many of its prime assets were in jeopardy, the situation symbolised by the state of the house itself, 'Bassetsbury Manor House being let to several poor families, is much out of repair and decreasing in value,' and of the two corn mills by the Manor House:

> The Mills are much in want of repair, and the foundations by no means secure, the repair of the buildings also has been much neglected. There is an excellent supply

of water, but if something considerable is not done soon, this estate cannot be expected to support the present value.

In addition, the Hedge Paper Mill 'is in want of repair'. However, to offset this depressing picture, Bridge and Loudwater Mills were reported as being in good repair and thriving (Loudwater Mill being a new replacement of the previous dilapidated one), and Oakridge Farm was also doing well.

The health of King's Wood, so vital to the economic health of the Manor in general, had unfortunately not improved, and the survey states:

> This wood is now very thin of oak and ash timber, and the beech are very small, it will be some years before it can produce a sale of beech timber owing to it having been so improperly cut. There may be an annual sale of thinnings in some parts of it, sufficient to pay the amount of the salary given to the person who has the care of it.

Bassetsbury still owned 'A small cottage and garden standing near the wood', and the report also mentions that, 'The whole of this wood is subject to the depasturage of cattle, which right is enjoyed in Common by those who reside near it and is an injury to the young timber.' More general remarks on the state of the wood follow:

> The boundary of this wood on one side is known only by some holes dug in the earth at very uncertain distances, and by marks on the respective trees which happen to grow near what they consider to be the division line, as these are likely to be cut down and the holes liable to be filled in, it certainly is necessary that stumps or something that is likely to be permanent should be placed down, and this I think should be done at the joint expense of the Dean & Canons and the proprietor of the adjoining wood.

The detailed surveys of the Manor begin to dry up from this time forward. The few reports that have survived dating to the mid–late 19th century show that the rot had truly set in and that this decline was irreversible and terminal, culminating in the final sale of the Manor's remaining assets towards the end of the century.

Maps became more frequent and detailed as the century progressed. One dating to 1832 shows little difference from the Totteridge of the 1770s. A few years later, though, it is evident that the settlement was beginning to grow. The 1840 map of the parish of Chepping Wycombe shows a community continuing to expand, as a few new buildings appeared, including White Cottage next to Totteridge Common and the dwelling that evolved into the Post Office and, later, Totteridge Stores (currently Ajantha's). The main road through the village was then called King's Wood Lane, and the development continued along the edge of this lane at the south end of the settlement, with the Common Cottages being constructed shortly after the

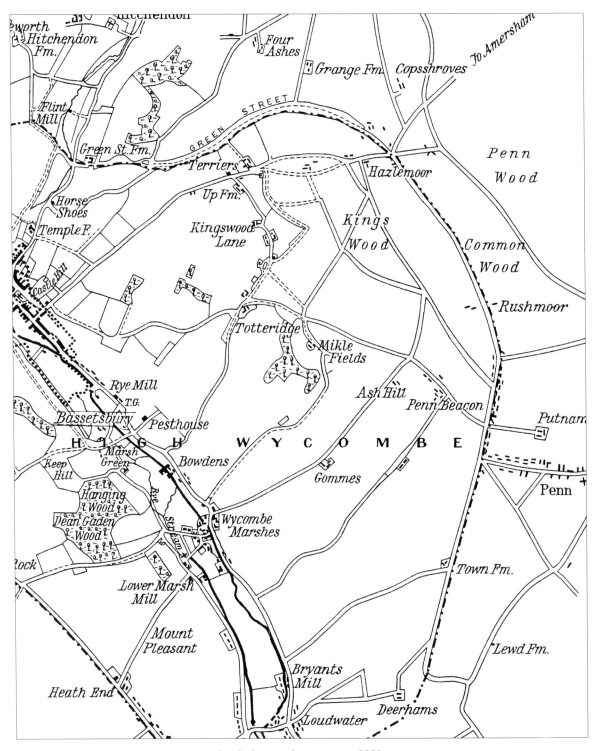

3 Ordnance Survey map, 1832.

map had been drawn up. Along the length of the valley bottom of King's Wood ran a well-trodden cleared pathway that still exists, although more overgrown, today.

Bricks and mortar alone cannot possibly reflect the complex and varied lives of the people who inhabited these buildings and it is the 1841 census of Wycombe and its environs that gives us our first detailed picture of the men, women and children of Totteridge, the official limits of which were defined as stretching from the beginning of King's Wood Lane at Terriers as far as Hicks Farm at the southern end. The village comprised 24 houses/residences containing a total of 85 people, of whom 62 were adults (15 years or over) and 23 were children. Of the 31 adult males, 20 are listed as being agricultural labourers, which is not unsurprising in an area containing four farms within a distance of a little over a mile. One of these labourers was John Bunce, aged 30, and his family had provided the name of Bunces Farm, which in the 20th century became known as Highfield Farm. As John Bunce is recorded as a labourer only, it is clear that the ownership of the farm lay elsewhere by this time, probably with John Young, who is recorded as a farmer (possibly of Little Totteridge Farm at Terriers) and is known to have sold the lease of Bunces Farm in 1854. One other 'farmer' is recorded, William Paine, who probably owned Hicks Farm. The census also mentions one chair-maker, Richard Hutchen aged 70; the wood bailiff, Thomas Dutton, who was employed by the Bassetsbury estate and resided in the cottage mentioned above; an army surgeon, George Rose of Totteridge House; and six adult males with no occupations listed. It is interesting to note in passing that the original Woodman's Cottage stood on the edge of Totteridge Common next to King's Wood until comparatively recent times, for it was demolished only in 1972 to make way for a new house which still bears the same name. Of the 31 adult females, the majority had no occupations listed. Two were recorded as agricultural labourers, one as a farm servant and one as a publican. The publican, of the *Dolphin*, was Ester Stallwood, aged 50, who lived in the pub with her children, Charlotte and Solomon, and her mother, Elizabeth, aged 80. The ages of the children, Charlotte at 20 and Solomon at 15, suggest that they assisted their mother in the running of the establishment in the apparent absence of their father.

The census finally brings us closer to our forebears, and it is easy to imagine the daily lives of these people. The population was well balanced and typical of its time and the occupations listed illustrate clearly that the economic base remained strongly agricultural. The next full census of the Wycombe area took place in 1851, and although the picture remains largely the same, the few differences begin to suggest how the community was starting to evolve. The area was now divided into Totteridge Lane and Totteridge and it is not clear where one ends and the other starts. The maps

4   White Cottage, with the *Dolphin*'s stable house in the background, *c.*1873-5.

of the region still show the geographical village limits extending from the site of Highworth Combined School to Hicks Farm, but it appears that the 1841 census limits, starting at Little Totteridge Farm at Terriers, were changed so that 'Totteridge Lane' was the area from Terriers to approximately 'Old Beams', and 'Totteridge' extended southwards from the *Dolphin*.

    'Totteridge Lane' consisted of 6 houses/residences containing a total of 27 people and 'Totteridge' contained 14 houses/residences with 68 people. Since 1841, the total recorded number of habitation sites had reduced from 24 to 20 although the number of inhabitants had increased from 85 to 95. In the 'official' Totteridge alone, the population of 68 was made up of 32 children and 36 adults, which not unsurprisingly displays the same balance of sexes (18 men and 18 women) as in 1841. The listed occupations have also remained largely the same. Of the men, 14 were agricultural labourers, Thomas Dutton (now 65) was still the wood bailiff,

Edwin Dutton (aged 25, Thomas' son?) was the 'woodman', there was one farm steward and one bricklayer's labourer. Of the women, Ester Stallwood was still at the *Dolphin*, there were four lacemakers, one housekeeper (at Totteridge House?), two official 'paupers', and ten recorded as having no occupation. An interesting point to note is that a child, James Hazel aged 13, was employed as a ploughboy, which, considering that he was the third of eight children and that his father was only an agricultural labourer, was an occupation no doubt forced upon the family through economic necessity.

One notable statistic from the 1851 census is the story of Caroline Russell. She was born in 1838 and in the census was recorded as being the 13-year-old daughter of George Russell and a scholar by occupation. Also living with the Russell family was their nephew, Frederick Bristow aged three. Hopping on many years, it was reported in the *Bucks Free Press* in 1921 that Caroline Bristow (née Russell) had died, but the name may be purely coincidental. She was remarked upon as being one of the oldest residents of Totteridge at the age of 83, having been married to James Bristow for over 60 years, and had started and ended her life in the same house.

What do all these statistics tell us and how had Totteridge really changed during these ten years? Hicks Farm appears to have been sold or leased, as the 1841 owner, William Paine, was no longer in residence, which meant that all of the three farms in the village (not including Little Totteridge Farm which had now become absorbed into Terriers) were now worked by tenant farmers. Over the ten-year period, only six families remained in the village, 17 had disappeared and 13 new families had arrived. Even though this may appear to be surprisingly similar to the late 20th-century experience, this image is fairly typical of mid-19th-century agricultural life, where the transitory and seasonal nature of the work resulted in employment that was rarely permanent. In the 19th century, lacemaking formed an important part of the rural life in the Wycombe area and, before the chair-making industry took off, constituted, along with paper-making, a major contributor to the economy of Chepping Wycombe. Indeed 'Buckinghamshire lace' was renowned throughout the country. The patterns were supplied by the large manufacturers and then passed to the lacemakers around the area, who traditionally conducted their craft on the thresholds of their cottages. This industry continued well into the 20th century and was a vital ingredient in the precarious economies of many small villages like Totteridge.

Chepping Wycombe was expanding in size and prosperity and all smaller rural settlements in the vicinity, known to the citizens of Wycombe town as 'The Foreigns', began to fall more within the influence of the town. To the

5   Farmland behind Bunces Farm, *c.*1870s.

north, the village of Hazlemere was growing as well and in 1847 Totteridge
was brought within its parish, two years after Holy Trinity, Hazlemere's first
church, had been built. Apparently, the inhabitants of Totteridge and other
local hamlets were regarded as uneducated and uncivilised, and in dire
need of spiritual guidance!

To all students of the history of Wycombe (and especially its brewing
past), the name of Wheeler will be very familiar. In the 19th century, the
Wheeler family was one of the most notable in Wycombe, being most
actively involved in brewing and banking, with members of the family
attaining the position of mayor 22 times during the century. In 1854,
some of the most prominent members of the family moved into Totteridge,
as Robert (a banker) and Thomas (a brewer) bought the lease of Bunces
Farm on 18 January from John Young of Little Totteridge Farm. The
lease commenced at Michaelmas 1853 and lasted for 21 years, at a rent
of £33 per annum. The details on the lease show that the farm consisted
of two cottages, gardens, an orchard, outbuildings, a barn, a stable and
other 'appurtenances'. The associated land consisted of several pieces of

FIRST EDITION.

HIGH WYCOMBE
AND GREAT MARLOW, BUCKS.

Particulars, Plans, and Conditions of Sale

Of the very valuable and important Freehold Properties, comprising the

BASSETSBURY MANOR ESTATE,

And including the

BASSETSBURY MANOR HOUSE, CORN MILL, FARM BUILDINGS, & LANDS,

THE "LOUDWATER" & "HEDGE MILL" PAPER MILLS

The extensive Beech Woodland known as

"KING'S WOOD,"

"OAKRIDGE" FARM AND WOOD,

A number of important

TRACTS OF BUILDING & FARM LANDS,

With WATER CRESS BEDS in or close to the Town of High Wycombe,

Five Old Established Public & Beerhouses,

The Site of the London Road Steam Saw Mills,

NUMEROUS CONVENIENT RESIDENCES AND COTTAGES,

PIECES OF MEADOW LANDS in Upper and Lower King's Meads, and

TWO VALUABLE PIECES OF BUILDING LAND,

Close to the Town of Great Marlow,

WHICH WILL BE OFFERED FOR SALE BY AUCTION, BY

Messrs. Vernon & Son,

AT THE RED LION HOTEL, HIGH WYCOMBE,

ON THURSDAY, JUNE 15TH, 1882,

At 2 for 3 o'clock in the Afternoon precisely,

By direction of the Ecclesiastical Commissioners for England (unless previously disposed of privately).

IN FORTY-TWO LOTS.

Early possession of every Lot may be obtained. The Properties may be viewed by permission of the respective tenants.

Particulars, with Plans and Conditions of Sale, may be obtained at the place of Sale, at the Auction Mart, Tokenhouse Yard, London, of Messrs. CLUTTON, 9, Whitehall Place, Westminster, Messrs. WHITE, BORRETT, & Co., Solicitors, 6, Whitehall Place, Westminster, and of Messrs. VERNON & SON, Land Agents, &c., 26, Great George Street, Westminster, and High Wycombe, Bucks.

W. BUTLER, PRINTER, 20, HIGH STREET, HIGH WYCOMBE.

6 Auction notice relating to the sale of the remaining assets of Bassetsbury Manor.

7   Totteridge Common and House at the turn of the century.

arable meadow and pasture totalling 21 acres, 2 rods and 26 poles, and the terms of the lease required the Wheelers to leave one-fifth of the land fallow and to tend the orchard. The farm was no doubt a very attractive small-holding, but today the obliteration of almost all traces of the site, approximately where the Tyzack Road bus-stop now stands, has unfortunately consigned this idyllic scene to the pages of history.

The High Wycombe Directory of 1875 gives us a further glimpse of life in the village. Although the total number of inhabitants is not recorded, it does list the various households and the name and occupation of each owner. Twenty-four people are mentioned, their professions including labourer (7), lacemaker (2), charwoman (1), gardener (1), farmer (1), cow-keeper (1), coachman (1), shoemaker (1), bricklayer (1), publican (1—William Putnam of the *Dolphin*), and Thomas John Reynolds of Totteridge House. It is encouraging to note that the remaining six

8 A postcard of King's Wood, late 19th century.

9 Totteridge Post Office at the turn of the century.

occupations listed are all involved in the furniture industry, for we have a timber-dealer, benchman, woodman, seat-maker, Windsor framer, and back-framer, illustrating the prominence the industry still enjoyed in the area at this time.

The life of the Manor of Bassetsbury finally came to an end towards the close of the 19th century. In the 1870s, the Manor was transferred from the Dean and Canons of St George's Chapel, Windsor, to the Ecclesiastical Commissioners, who took over direct control when the Dashwood family's lease of the Manor expired in about 1880. The Ecclesiastical Commissioners then decided to break up and dispose of all their landed estates in Wycombe, with the exception of some unenclosed waste ground which included Tylers Green, Flackwell Heath, Marsh Green, Keep Hill and a part of Totteridge Common. On 15 June 1882, the remaining assets of Bassetsbury Manor were auctioned off. These included Loudwater Mill, Hedge Mill, the Manor House with its mill and other buildings, Oakridge Farm and wood, and land both at King's Meads and more local to the Manor House, with associated buildings. King's Wood was also included in the sale and it was purchased for £5,000 by Sir Philip Rose, who at that time owned Totteridge House together with large tracts of land in Totteridge. The adjacent St John's Wood was not included in the sale, having been enclosed earlier in 1869.

The end of the century saw the village becoming more incorporated into the general community of Wycombe. Hazlemere had already developed into a thriving village with its own church, and in the early 1890s it was decided that Totteridge needed its own centre of worship. The third vicar of Hazlemere, the Reverend James Morgan West, was becoming increasingly concerned about the level of education in his parish, which evidently had not progressed too far in the forty years since the establishment of Holy Trinity, and so the building of St Andrew's Mission Church in Totteridge began. It is reported that the church took an unusually long time to complete, testing the vicar's patience to the limit, but it was finally completed in 1894 once the fund set up by the Rev. West had received the required £230. The church was built on land donated by Sir Philip Rose on the site adjacent to the current Totteridge Lane/Drive intersection, with the services being shared between the Rev. West and Mr. H. Young, a lay preacher.

Queen Victoria's Diamond Jubilee year was in 1897, and on 22 June celebrations took place nationwide. Terriers Common was the venue for the inhabitants of the area and the event was celebrated with fireworks and, among others activities, a tug-of-war competition between Totteridge and Hazlemere. Totteridge won by two pulls to one! A map dated to 1898 shows clearly how the area was changing. Development in Totteridge had well and

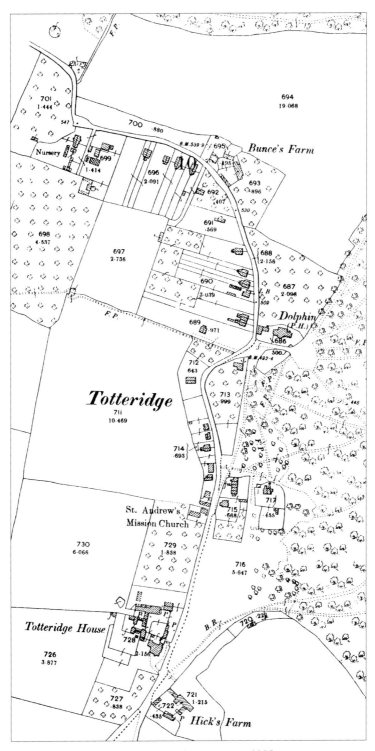

10 Ordnance Survey map, 1898.

11   Cherry pickers in Totteridge, late 19th century.

12 Totteridge Common, *c.*1910.

truly started, with houses now built along much of the west side of Totteridge Lane between the Post Office and the site of Highworth Combined School. In 1893 Dupont Cottages were constructed next to the Post Office. Chair-making at this time had become one of the main industries of Wycombe and it seems that King's Wood, being a major source for the industry, was bringing its rewards to the locality. The century closed and the prosperity of Totteridge seemed assured.

Four

THE 20TH CENTURY
FROM OPULENCE TO OBSCURITY

At the beginning of the 20th century, Totteridge had all the trappings of a country village: a pub, a church, a prestigious country house and a thriving economy based primarily on agriculture. One of the prime routes into the village was up Totteridge Hill (now Road) which at this time was just a stony track across farmland belonging to Bowerdean Farm in the valley below and to Totteridge Farm at the top end. Up on the ridge, further development was in progress as plots began to be marked out and large houses, including the imposing Hill House (situated in a two-acre plot known as Hill House Estate), were being built. Also at about this time, Hatters Lane was properly metalled to cater for the increase in vehicular traffic requiring access to London Road. It is said that the first car in Totteridge was seen *c.*1905 and caused great excitement among the local children. At the other end of the village, Barton Lodge was built on the derelict site of the former Little Totteridge House (now the site of Highworth Combined School) and, a short way off, the brewer Robert Wheeler had in 1904 moved into St John's House at Terriers. As Wycombe grew, Totteridge became more attractive to settlers.

In 1913, just before the First World War broke out, the town of Wycombe was embroiled in a conflict of its own. A dispute had arisen in the furniture industry over rates of pay and a union formed which quickly resulted in the majority of workers going on strike. The dominance of the industry in the area meant hardship for the town while the dispute lasted, but fortunately agreement was reached in early 1914. By the time the war started later in the year, the industry had settled once more and began to concentrate on assisting the war effort, although with a greatly depleted workforce due to enlistment. King's Wood played its part, for the trees on the east side of the wood were cut down and used as pit-props in the trenches of France, while the tree tops were left on the ground for people to take away as firewood. Even today, very few mature trees exist in this part of the wood, as the clearance and replanting of the area did not take place until the early 1950s. It is reported that during the war years the sight of Wycombe inhabitants trundling down Totteridge Hill with barrows, prams, etc. laden with logs and brushwood from King's Wood was commonplace.

13   Totteridge Lane looking towards Terriers, *c.*1909.

14   Totteridge Lane and Post Office, *c.*1913.

Totteridge suffered its share of sorrow during the war. Twenty local men were reported to have joined up but, unfortunately, not all survived. The casualties included Herbert Putnam, the youngest of three sons all of whom joined the army, and also Pte. Percy Aldridge of the Wycombe Battalion of the Bucks. Territorials, who was killed in France in 1916 and died in the presence of Pte. Jack Mines, a local man who had married Percy's sister. A memorial stone in St Andrew's Mission Church recorded the names of other Totteridge men who fell during the Great War, including Victor Gregson, Samual Kibble (no doubt related to the Kibble family who ran Hicks and Hatters Farms) and George Moore (who was a manager of the St Andrew's Room at the church). The memorial stone was rescued when St Andrew's was demolished in 1978 and can now be seen in St Francis' Church at Terriers. The vicar of the parish at the time was Rev. C.H.Clissold and he contributed to the war effort by becoming a war chaplain in France.

15   The development of Totteridge Hill, with Bowerdean Farm in the foreground, 1928.

The years immediately after the war were the last of any relative peace for the quiet village. In the early 1920s, flower traders from London used to arrive at Wycombe on the 6a.m. workers' train, run up the stony Totteridge Hill with sacks in their hands, and collect as many oxeye daisies as time and space would allow from the fields around the current Elora Road. Then, they rushed to catch the next train back to London, to start selling the flowers by 8a.m. London Friendly Societies often visited Wycombe by train at this time, and travelled up to Totteridge, sometimes accompanied by a band encouraging them up the challenging hill, to spend the day on and around Totteridge Common. Known colloquially as 'Beanfeasters', this annual outing was for many poorer families the only opportunity they had to escape from the city and spend a relaxing day in the country. Some of the local children even took the opportunity to earn a few pennies by selling the visitors bunches of flowers picked from their gardens. The period also saw the occasional game of cricket being enjoyed on the Common. However, this idyllic rural scene was destined not to last long.

The period 1910-20 saw the population of Wycombe starting to expand rapidly and with this came the inevitable demand for more housing. Pressure to act had been on the Council for some time and they applied to the government for the necessary resources, which were eventually forthcoming shortly after the end of the war. In 1919 the housing estate at Terriers formed part of the first wave of new development, and this was followed in 1925-6 by the largest and most ambitious development project yet attempted in Wycombe, the Bowerdean Farm Estate. In the late 1920s, over 500 houses were built throughout the Bowerdean valley, spreading up the hill to link the outskirts of Wycombe to the new housing at the south edge of Totteridge. A well-known local builder involved with this project was Mr. James Bond of Totteridge Avenue (Builder, Undertaker & House Decorator)!

In 1921 there was a proposal by the current owner of King's Wood, Edward Wootton Dean (timber merchant), that the wood be clear-felled. Not surprisingly, there was immediate local outrage, resulting in the wood being offered to the Corporation of High Wycombe for the sum of £1,000, to be used as a public open space. The Corporation initially wished to develop the wood for housing but, as this was not permitted and they could not afford the costs of maintaining the open space, the purchase was not made. Several other parties then expressed their interest in the wood and Chepping Wycombe Parish Council became involved, seeking to secure the purchase themselves in order to protect the wood from development. However, they were able to afford only £700 and advised that the balance be raised locally. Eventually, more than £250 was donated locally and the wood was purchased for £850, negotiated down from the original £1,000. Such was the local desire to preserve the wood that the schoolchildren of Tylers Green donated their pennies and even some silver coins. The sale was completed on 5 August 1922 and included Totteridge Common and other small areas adjoining King's Wood (including the land below the *Dolphin*). This event marked the end of the wood's use as a serious independent economic asset. The wood was opened up fully to public use, although the Parish Council has continued to the present day to manage the wood successfully and use its crop to fund the ongoing maintenance costs of this ancient and valuable area. The former privileges of allowing animals to graze and forage in the wood and on the common were maintained by the Council, ending only in 1976 when the rights of recreation only were permitted. In 1923 the first warden of King's Wood, Mr. George, was appointed, and he started his duties by clearing away the broken glass and crockery. The same year also saw the wood's first by-laws set.

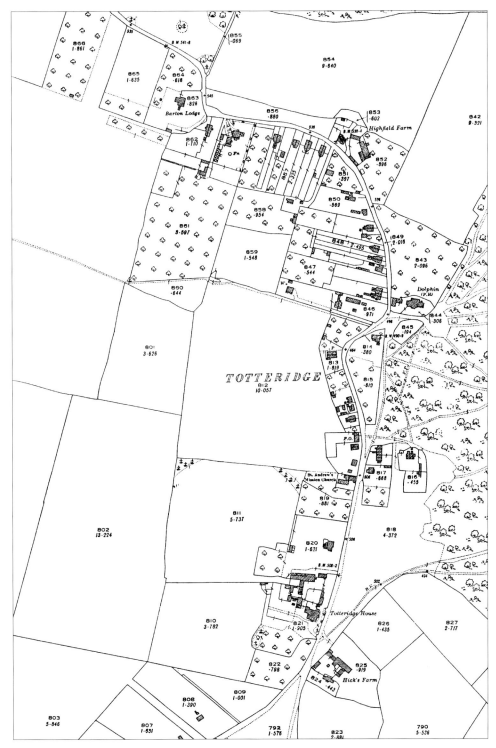

16 Ordnance Survey map, 1925.

A detailed map of 1925 shows that more changes were taking place in the village itself. A few more houses had been built along the west side of Totteridge Lane and Bunces Farm had changed its name to Highfield Farm, later known locally as Tuckers Farm after Jack Tucker who owned it and whose family had lived in the area for many generations. 1925 also saw the new water mains being extended from the main village through Hicks Farm, to serve the new estate being developed at the top of Hatters Lane.

The pace of development increased in the years before the Second World War. In January 1929, Terriers School was opened by the mayor of Wycombe, Councillor A. Stacey, and was designed to accommodate two hundred children from both Totteridge and Terriers. In the early 1930s The Crescent was begun, with its adjoining Drives (North, South, East, West and New) linking into the Bowerdean Farm Estate. Before The Crescent was started, the land at the lower end of the site, by the current Uplands Close, was occupied by

17   The laying of the foundation stone of Terriers School, 18 July 1928.

a poultry farm of about four acres run by the Line family (later taken over by the Simmons family, when pigs were added). In *c.*1930 the new Post Office opened up on Totteridge Hill, taking over the function from the shop in the heart of the village, which continued to exist as a general store (although still selling stamps), run by Mrs. J. Plumridge. Also in the 1930s, the houses of Hardenwaye were constructed on the site of the paddock belonging to Old Beams, and houses were built above the *Dolphin* and below Hicks Farm. Between 1925 and 1934 Hill House was owned by Charles Colston (the managing director of Hoover in London, who went on to start his own electrical business at Wycombe Marsh), who purchased much of the land between Hill House and the edge of Micklefield to allay the threat of development. At this time the southern edge of Totteridge boasted many impressive elm trees, a small stream that trickled down towards Micklefield, and several small and attractive ponds. Further into the village and adjacent to the *Dolphin* was 'Ingledell', a house with its own orchard, bounded by the original loop of the lane and inhabited by Miss A. Ball, who was reputed to have been a high-society fashion model in the 1920s and '30s. In Kingswood View lived and worked possibly one of the last local chair-makers, Mr. J. Aldridge.

The population increase attracted several small businesses to the area. On the site where Wynbury Drive now starts, the Putnams were running the family butcher business, with its own abattoir to the rear, and Aubrey Clinch was running a small bakery in New Drive, adjacent to Mr. Robinson the butcher and Mrs. Harker the grocer. In Mountain Ash Stores beyond Old Beams, Miss C. Salter was operating her own small general store from premises that had been in the Salter family since they were first built in the early 1900s. Miss Salter is remembered as having issued rations to the village during the Second World War, but a more dramatic tale surrounds the site. During the war, a male Polish assistant called Jan helped to run the store, and when Miss Salter died unmarried in the late 1940s she left the premises to her helper, who moved in with his wife. The Pole had a terrible temper though, and the sounds of domestic unrest often disturbed the otherwise tranquil neighbourhood. Shortly afterwards, the wife is reported to have 'disappeared' and this was followed by another Polish man coming to stay at the house. Tempers continued to flare and the Pole attacked his friend with an axe. Eventually, the Pole shot himself and also tried to burn the house down! The turbulent history of the house thankfully ended there and all has been peaceful since.

In 1938 Totteridge was still an independent village in its own right, although seriously threatened by development from both ends. The Common was still used for the occasional game of cricket and was also the venue in August for the Bowerdean Children's Treat. In King's Wood a fire was reported to have destroyed four acres, and the squirrel problem had become

18 The view up Totteridge Hill, *c.*1930.

so acute that shoots had to be organised to control the pest, an event that continued for many years afterwards. Hatters Lane School on the borders of Totteridge was opened on Saturday 14 October 1939 by Alderman W.H. Tyzack and its first headmaster was Stan Perfect who had moved down from Terriers School and lived in The Crescent.

For most of the 20th century, Totteridge has boasted its own football club, still active in the Sunday Combination, but perhaps the largest single

19 The top of Totteridge Road, showing Hicks Farm, *c.*1930.

contribution to the sporting life of the village took place in 1939 when Ernest Turner's Sports Ground opened. Ernest Turner's Electrical Instruments, based in Totteridge Avenue, was a world leader in its field, and at Christmas 1937 the owner rashly promised his employees that he would build them a sports ground. Being a man of his word, the ground was duly opened on 3 June 1939 by the Lord Lieutenant of Buckinghamshire. The ground, which included tennis courts and a bowling green, was partially

20   Totteridge Lane below the *Dolphin*, 1935.

financed by the King George V Jubilee Playing Fields Fund and for many years thereafter was used primarily for cricket and football, also boasting the first electronic scoreboard to be introduced into Buckinghamshire. Several village fêtes were also hosted at the ground after this privilege had passed with the land from Totteridge House. These annual fêtes became very elaborate affairs, with athletics (including on occasions semi-professional track racing and boxing), sack races, dancing, coconut shies, a grand marquee for tea, and were normally rounded off by an impressive firework display.

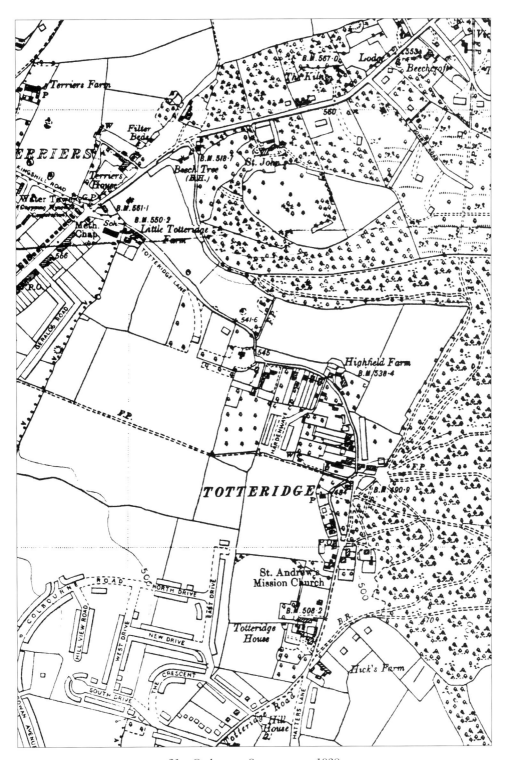

21 Ordnance Survey map, 1938.

22   Ernest Turner's Sports Club First XI football team, 1951-2.

The sports ground was eventually sold off by Ernest's son, Norman, in the 1980s to Wycombe Hills Squash Club and in the early 1990s was developed into Turner's Drive and, later, Lyndon Gardens.

When war broke out in 1939, Totteridge was fortunate enough to escape the more serious effects of the conflict. The first bomb in the area fell by the southern edge of King's Wood close to the pair of cottages known jointly as Found Out, but the bomb never exploded. However, on the warm evening of 19 June 1944, another bomb, believed to have been a doodlebug (or 'buzz bomb'), came to earth and exploded on farmland between Totteridge and Terriers close to Redford's playing field and the Royal Grammar School, badly damaging many buildings in the vicinity. As well as blowing in no fewer than 52 windows of the Royal Grammar School, the blast cracked the walls of Highfield Farm and also caused structural damage as far away as the new houses of The Crescent and the shops on Totteridge Hill! Fortunately, there were no casualties. Around the verges of Totteridge, at the bottom end of Hatters Lane at Pinions, a Mosquito crashed into the railway embankment just next to the bridge, and a short way off, in Four Ashes, another bomb fell in a field close to Brands House, the crater of which remains impressively large even today. King's Wood was used for military manoeuvres, primarily by the Home Guard who dug many trenches, as well as for amorous manoeuvres, primarily by American GIs 'getting to know' the local girls!

The agricultural community stoutly supported the war effort and POWs were brought in to help work the farmland in the village and continue the building of Totteridge Drive and adjacent roads. Although most of the POWs occupied other parts of the Wycombe area, some Italians were based for a short time at St John's House in Terriers. In addition, many locals not directly employed in agriculture helped out with the 'Dig for Victory' call and allotments were opened up close to the Common. Evacuated families, primarily from the Hammersmith area of London, moved into the area and Terriers School, under the headmaster Mr. Thomas, took on the additional children. The morning classes were initially dedicated to the local children and the afternoon ones to the evacuees, who also had gardening lessons in the kitchen garden of Totteridge House. Eventually, as the war progressed and the number of evacuees increased, any suitable space in the village was used as classrooms. Adjacent to Terriers School stood Little Totteridge Farm, run by Tom 'Pop' Smith, who often became so incensed with balls continually coming onto his land that he eventually prevented all returns!

In 1940, a local tragedy hit the small community. Amos Putnam, who lived in Hatters Lane and ran the family butcher's business close to the *Dolphin*, committed suicide in his own slaughter-house at the age of 68 because of worries about the meat rationing and fears that his business would not survive. He had been a butcher in the area for well over forty years and was remembered as being 'the happiest man in the world' before the war. After Amos' death, his son Ron took over the business.

Hicks Farm was run by the Kibble family under Leonard, with the help of his father John (known as Albert) Kibble. Albert, an old man at the time, delivered the milk in the area on his bicycle when his daughter Cath, whose job it usually was, joined the Women's Land Army. The Kibble family was very prominent in Totteridge at this time, also being the owners of Hatters Farm, which was run primarily by Albert. Albert,

23   The gallant men of Totteridge ARP, outside the *Dolphin*.

who possessed a hook in the place of one hand, was the Superintendent of the afternoon Sunday School at St Andrew's and was reputed never to have never missed a service. He died in 1941 aged 86 and the farms continued under Len, who had a very different reputation from his father. Len was apparently a bit of a 'lad about town' and was well known for his passion for beer and the ladies. He claimed that he took to beer after a tornado had removed the roof of a house in Wendover he had been in, and he needed the beer to wash away the memory! His fondness for the brew was such that he regularly had to be carted home from the *Black Boy* at Terriers. Another tale alleges that he was once spotted climbing out of a back-bedroom window of a lady friend as her husband was coming through the front door!

Totteridge survived the war relatively unscathed. Immediately after, there was a huge demand for council houses and they were needed quickly.

24   The children of Totteridge celebrating VE Day outside the Ernest Turner SC pavilion.

Traditional building material was in very short supply and the solution was the manufacture of mainly pre-fabricated structures. On the edge of the village, in the fields behind Hardenwaye, about 100 steel-framed and partially steel-clad houses were erected, mainly in the area around The Quadrant and the east end of Totteridge Drive. It is a testament to the builders of the time that a great many of these houses are still standing and occupied today.

The late 1940s saw the start of the greatest changes ever to have affected Totteridge. The sudden influx of new residents into Totteridge Drive hastened the development of the estate further eastwards across the fields, to join up eventually with Bowerdean in the late 1950s, by which time the development around The Crescent area, somewhat hindered by the war, was completed. In 1948 Aubrey Clinch retired from the bakery in New Drive and the Mayo family took over. However, perhaps the most poignant symbol of the changes in the village at this time is the tale of Highfield Farm. In the 1940s the arable farm was occupied by George and Sylvia Scott and the land rented to them by the Clays, who owned Barton Lodge and much of the land at the north end of the village. Dick Clay had been a director of Broomwade's and a town councillor in the 1930s and '40s, and when land came up for sale

25 Happier days—the children of Totteridge and Terriers at Terriers School, May Day 1948.

before the war, he bought up as much as he could to protect it from further development. At the heart of this ancient part of Totteridge stood Highfield Farm, believed to be at least 400 years old, the residence not only of the Scotts but also another mysterious occupant. In the early 1940s, the Scott's eldest daughter, Jacynth, just a toddler at the time, fell into the habit of chatting to and laughing with an 'invisible friend' in the fields around the farmhouse. When questioned, she spoke of her friendly Pink Lady, named after the long flowing pink dress that she always wore that would sweep

26 A painting of Hicks Farm by E. Leeder, early 1950s.

elegantly across the grass whenever she moved. Nobody else could see the lady and so the story was more or less dismissed as childhood fancy. However, until she was about five or six, Jacynth continued to see the sociable apparition, which slowly moved into the garden and eventually into the farmhouse itself, favouring the sitting-room. Although no other witnesses ever saw the mysterious Pink Lady, the atmosphere inside the house in the late 1940s was described as intensely happy, warm and welcoming, especially noticeable when returning home.

Dick Clay died of a heart attack in the early 1950s and his widow sold Barton Lodge and all its land, including Highfield Farm, to the Council. There was initially a plan formulated by Broomwade's to put a sports ground on the land but this never came to fruition, the Council beginning development after less than one year. Highfield Farm was completely demolished, along with Little Totteridge and Hicks Farms, and the Pink Lady was never seen again. The ancient and intimate soul of Totteridge had been bulldozed away.

27   The Coronation Party for the children of The Crescent and The Drives, held in a barn belonging to Simmons' pig and poultry farm, June 1953.

Within a few years, Totteridge was transformed into the settlement we know today. In 1954 Totteridge Lane was widened starting from the north end, and the former crossroads at Terriers became the staggered junction, which necessitated the demolition of a house on the site of the car-park. Fremantle Road was started and, further down below Barton Lodge, the new road was straightened, cutting directly across the Highfield Farm fields to link up with the new Tyzack Road development (named after Alderman W.H.Tyzack who had served on the Wycombe Town Council for many years). Below the *Dolphin* the road was also straightened, cutting across the site of 'Ingledell' which had already been demolished following a few years of dereliction. At the time of the demolition, it is said that a plague of crickets infested the area! The estate across the fields to the west of Totteridge expanded quickly from Totteridge Drive, eventually linking up to the new Terriers housing estate by 1960, and Hicks Farm Rise was developed after the compulsory purchase and demolition of the farm, linking into the new estate at Micklefield. In the late 1950s, the Hill House Estate was in the ownership of Philip Eldridge, the

28 Miss Elsie Carter, King's Wood County First School's first head teacher.

builder, and he began selling off several plots surrounding the house for development into individual residences. The *Golden Fleece* public house was built at the same time by Benskins Brewery of Watford. To the south, Hatters Lane continued to spread its branches, from Wingate Avenue (completed in the late 1940s) to those roads commemorating the 1953 conquest of Everest (Hillary Road, Hunt Road, Tenzing Drive and Everest Road). Another victim of the population expansion at this time was Hatters Farm above Hatters Lane School. Totteridge had become enveloped by building works on all sides except the east, where King's Wood alone stood firm against expansion, but the heart of the village remained relatively untouched, the only major change there being the opening on 2 October 1950 of King's Wood County First School (now King's Wood Infant School) on land formerly owned by Totteridge Farm.

The school was founded as an Infant School for 280 children and it was officially opened on 22 January 1951 by Mrs. C.R. Attlee, the wife of the prime minister. The first headteacher was the popular Miss Elsie

29   A rare occurrence—seven sets of twins attended King's Wood County First School in the 1950s.

Carter, who was progressive enough to nurture on her staff the first male teacher of an infants' school in the area, David Cox. The First School immediately took over from Terriers School as the main centre of education for the children of Totteridge, and achieved some local fame in the late 1950s when no less than seven sets of twins attended the school at the same time. In 1957 the school was extended to cope with the rapidly expanding local population, mainly from the new Hicks Farm estate, but even this was not enough. The situation continued to worsen so that in 1964 two classes had to relocate to the premises of the Totteridge and District Social Club in Totteridge Drive. The pressure was finally eased when, on 18 October 1968, King's Wood County Junior School in Hollis Road was officially opened by Prof. C.C. Butler (Dean of the Royal College of Science). The school was almost named Hicks Farm School in memory of the farm on whose land it stood but the majority voted for King's Wood (suggested by Elsie Carter) in order to forge closer links with the First School established several years previously. The first headmaster was John R. Veysey and eight teachers moved across

30   Pupils at King's Wood County First School in the 1950s.

immediately from the First School. Shortly after its foundation, temporary classrooms were added and in 1974 a double-block of four permanent classrooms was built, by which time the school had become known as the County Middle School (now King's Wood Junior School).

The Hollis Road development in the late 1950s was a significant contribution to the life of the village. Not only did it bring much-needed additional educational facilities to the community in the form of the Secondary School, it also provided the site for St Wulfstan's Catholic Church, built in 1969 and consecrated on 30 April 1970. Senior pupils from King's Wood County Junior School made a significant contribution to the new church by designing a 56 sq.ft. decorated tiled floor depicting marine life. The church was named after St Wulfstan, who came to High Wycombe in *c.*1076 when he was Bishop of Worcester and consecrated All Saints' Church, in which a statue of Wulfstan can still be seen. St Wulfstan's Church

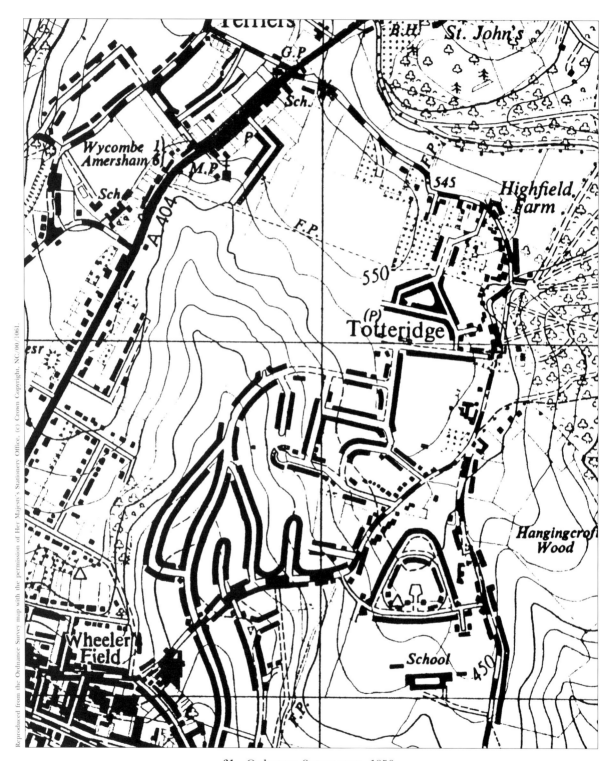

31 Ordnance Survey map, 1950.

underwent major rebuilding during 1991 after suffering serious structural problems, and since then has continued to serve the religious needs of the community with its new capacity of one hundred and fifty parishioners. Also at this time the church sold some of its adjacent land and on 3 August 1992 the purpose-built Kingswood Surgery opened on the site.

Two other churches appeared in Totteridge in the middle of the century. The earlier was Totteridge Baptist Church, which was opened on 1 April 1950 in what was to become Hillary Road, as a part of the expansion of the Union Baptist Church in the Wycombe area. The original plot chosen for the church was located opposite the eventual site but was abandoned owing to the slope of the ground. An organ, purchased from Luton, was installed for the opening, and several years later a church hall was added. Around the corner in Hatters Lane, in March 1961, St Andrew's Church was officially dedicated by the Bishop of Oxford. St Andrew's was founded in 1897 as a mission church next to the new school in Gordon Road and there it remained for many decades. However, because of an increasing population and the North Town area's being zoned for industrial development after the Second World War, it was decided to relocate the church. In 1959 the Hatters Lane site was decided upon, partly in order to serve the new population of the Hicks Farm Estate.

In the early 1960s, the lane below the *Dolphin* was straightened after the destruction of a house on the necessary land and the infilling of a large hollowed area with rubble which included demolished air-raid shelters. One of these had been located on Totteridge Green and constructed in 1941. It was fortunate for the village that a planning application for a petrol station next to the road below the pub was refused in 1965. Only a few major changes have occurred since the 1950s and '60s. Wynbury Drive was built in the 1960s, which necessitated the demolition of three houses along the edge of Totteridge Lane, including Putnam's butcher's shop. In 1972 Barton Lodge, owned by the council, was demolished to make way for Terriers Middle School (now Highworth Combined School). Some of this fine Edwardian residence's character still lingers, for many of the garden's fruit trees have been retained in the grounds of the school and some of the brick-and-flint boundary wall remains bordering the plot. Also in 1972, the original Woodman's Cottage, nestling on the edge of Totteridge Common next to King's Wood, was demolished to make way for the construction of a new house that still goes by the same name.

Totteridge was now well served by all facilities and had been ruthlessly incorporated into the ever-expanding High Wycombe. The boundaries of the village became more blurred, illustrated by the incorporation of the majority of Totteridge in 1973 into the parish of St Francis' Church at

32   The original Woodman's Cottage, mid-1960s.

Terriers (completed in 1929). St Andrew's Mission Church continued for a few more years, but was eventually sold in 1978 and demolition followed shortly afterwards. It was a great loss, for St Andrew's had faithfully served the community since 1894 and had formed the spiritual heart of the village, its church hall at the rear hosting innumerable village functions, including regular use as a venue for Chepping Wycombe Parish Council meetings. In 1899 the hall (St Andrew's Room) was even used for an 'Optical Lantern Entertainment'! It was the main social centre of Totteridge and during the 1930s held many popular events which included concerts and whist drives. It had a very active Youth Club (started by Eileen Howse in 1946) and Sunday School and became the regular venue for the Totteridge Lads' Social Club and the mothers-and-babies clinic. Although burnt down in 1946, the

33   St Andrew's Mission Church, *c*.1904.

hall was promptly rebuilt to continue its faithful service. It was not unusual for the occasional open-air service to be held on the adjacent Totteridge Common. The last service held in the church was, appropriately, on St Andrew's Day in November 1977. After the demolition, the church bell, which had famously been struck by lightning, was taken to a mission church in Nigeria, the organ went to Eye church in Suffolk (where it is still used by its owners, the Eye Bach Choir), while other articles, including the altar-rails, a cross, a bookstand, a portable font, candle-holders, a sanctuary light and the First World War memorial, ended up in St Francis' at Terriers.

The late 20th century saw little further major change. The boundaries of King's Wood were eroded away even more, mainly on the north and east sides towards Hazlemere and Tylers Green, in the interests of housing development. Within Totteridge itself, minor development continued at the south end, including the brief appearance of Wycombe Hills Squash Club in the playing field that was formerly Turners' Sports Ground, now transformed into Lyndon Gardens. At the north end, Kingswood Place was built behind Highworth School in 1998-9. In March 2000, the local parish boundaries altered once more, those parts of Totteridge not included in the

1973 boundary change (Tyzack Road, Rushbrooke Close, Larkfield Close, St Andrews Close and the even-numbered houses of Totteridge Lane) being transferred from the parish of Hazlemere to the parish of St Francis at Terriers.

At the very beginning of the new millennium occurred one of the saddest events to have hit the area in recent times. On the night of 31 January 2000, the empty Terriers First School, built in 1928, was targeted by arsonists. The damage was so extensive that complete demolition was inevitable, and this was eventually completed in June. The site had been closed down as a functioning school on 20 May 1997, its children relocated to Highworth Combined School. Although the original plan had been to reopen the building as a school for special-needs children, the site is scheduled (in October 2000) to be redeveloped for even more housing.

The village of Totteridge was finally recognised by Wycombe District Council in 1986 when it designated the village a Conservation Area, thereby dignifying it as an 'area of special architectural or historical interest considered worthy of preservation or enhancement', in which strict controls on building alterations are enforced. The Area covers the former heart of Totteridge, from the *Dolphin* southwards to the edge of the Richard Gardens development, including Totteridge Common and the more prominent buildings within the boundaries such as the *Dolphin*, the Common Cottages, Dupont Cottages and the former Post Office, White Cottage, Totteridge House and Totteridge Farm House. It is perhaps surprising that the oldest house in Totteridge, Old Beams, has been excluded from the area. To the north, Terriers has also been designated a Conservation Area, incorporating the *Beech Tree* public house, Terriers House and the linear field running adjacent to Totteridge Lane. Both villages finally have the official protection they deserve.

What is Totteridge now, at the beginning of the 21st century? The geographical boundaries have become somewhat obscured and ill-defined through development, but can broadly be regarded as extending along the length of Totteridge Lane and then eastwards across the top of the hill, the area limits defined by the edges of the ridge as the housing starts to blend into Bowerdean and Terriers to the west and north, and Hatters Lane and Hicks Farm Rise to the south and east. The former village still exists in essence, not only in the buildings themselves but also in the inhabitants, many of whom have spent most of their lives in the area and remember with clarity and affection the days when Totteridge was a small, unique and friendly community. The mid-20th-century development has attracted a new established community who form the revitalised social heart of the area, revolving largely around the schools, the *Dolphin,* and the ever-active

Totteridge and District Social Club (built with the estate in the 1950s) and the Totteridge Arts and Drama Society.

The history of Totteridge reflects the evolution of both the town in the valley below as well as the country in general. No historical fireworks were ever ignited in Totteridge and in that respect the village can be safely regarded as typical of so many other thousands of similar communities around Britain. The individual character of the settlement can still be identified by those willing to look, but the general feeling that the area is merging into High Wycombe and developing into an urban suburb is becoming increasingly prevalent. The ridge of Totteridge has been occupied for many centuries (and possibly millennia) and it would be a tragedy if short-term development was allowed to obliterate such unique memories.

I can think of no better epitaph to the past life of the village than the poignant and sad words of Joan Keen, written in 1981:

Ode to Totteridge

Do you remember Totteridge, long ago?
A little village with a winding lane,
Where everyone you met, you used to know,
And we all felt our neighbours' joy or pain.
An old one died—why, the whole village mourned;
In each new baby, we all seemed to share;
The little shops—Miss Salter's—'Mrs. Jim's'
And our own butcher—Putman's was there.
Kingswood was green, and clean and litter free,
The Coppice pond, where squirrels drank, was clear.
The neighbours visited, and talked, and helped;
And all our social life was centred here.
Where farms and fields were once, estates stand now;
A road has taken over the lane,
And people often pass without a nod,
And don't care if they ever meet again.
Our local inn, the *Dolphin*, still is here,
And there's a core of the old Totteridge yet
Who still remember what the village was ...
Remember—and regret.

Five

SITES OF SPECIAL INTEREST

This final chapter serves as an appendix to the tale of Totteridge and provides a more detailed insight into three of the more prominent and historic sites in the village: Totteridge House and Farm, the *Dolphin* public house, and Old Beams. The nature of the community through the ages and consequent shortage of records has meant that these histories are incomplete and many gaps exist which may never be filled. The facts that have been uncovered, though, help us to envisage with greater clarity the lives of the people who struggled to ensure that Totteridge survived and grew into the settlement we know today.

Totteridge House and Farm

Totteridge House is still the most imposing building in the village. Nestling quietly behind trees opposite Totteridge Common, its weathered brickwork and towering chimneys are a clear indication that this was once a residence of substance and wealth. It is believed to be (and officially recorded as) 17th-century in origin, but much altered in the 19th, although the original builder and inhabitant remains unknown. It is possible that a house called King's Wood House once stood on the site, occupied by Constantine Slater in 1584 (see Chapter 2), but no conclusive evidence for this remains. Totteridge House itself seems to have been constructed at a time when Totteridge consisted of only a few farms and other isolated houses. Its construction and the arrival of a wealthy family would certainly have been a major event in the history of the community and signified to the Wycombe area that Totteridge was becoming a more desirable place to live. It is likely that the house was built independently of Bassetsbury Manor which at this time was in decline.

The history of the house in the 17th and 18th centuries remain vague but we can conjecture some of its story from later facts. Throughout the 19th and into the 20th centuries, the Rose family, originally from Thame, are known to have inhabited Totteridge House. It is also known that the first Rose, Thomas, moved into Wycombe in the early 18th century, later becoming Mayor. Thomas's residence in the area is not recorded although it is very possible that he did purchase (and maybe even build) Totteridge House. The Rose family were exceptionally successful in Wycombe, Thomas's son, Thomas, becoming in his turn Mayor of Wycombe three times in the latter half of the 18th century, and his third son, William, also later becoming Mayor. Such an important family would no doubt have occupied a prestigious and imposing residence.

Totteridge Farm (on the site of the current Reynolds Close) is likely to have been built at the same time as, or soon after, the foundation of the house itself. One of the oldest buildings associated with the farm and still virtually untouched is Totteridge House Cottage, dated to the 18th century. The farm's land extended west across the edge of the ridge until it met the property of Bowerdean Farm, with Hicks Farm owning the land in the opposite direction across Totteridge Lane. The earliest map which defines the site with any clarity dates to 1840 and shows a variety of structures which would have been utilitarian farm buildings as well as homes to a few farm labourers.

The 1841 census identifies the inhabitant of Totteridge House as George Rose (aged 50) and records his profession as Army Surgeon. The census taken in 1851 shows that no member of the Rose family was inhabiting the house, although it was still in the family's hands. In 1861 the house was the property of Philip Rose Esq. (a lawyer working in London) of Rayners, and the residence of Charles Fowler. The large house of Rayners in Penn (now occupied by Penn School) was built by Philip in 1847 and Philip's son, Philip, records later that during the construction of Rayners, 'my Father rented a House about 2 miles distant at Totteridge, a House which he subsequently purchased with the Farm attached to it.' This clearly casts doubt on whether the Rose family actually owned Totteridge House prior to the mid-19th century, although the presence of George Rose in 1841 suggests that a branch of the family did own the property and that Philip's purchase was conducted within the family.

Philip's legal career flourished, and in 1874 he became Sir Philip Rose, 1st Baronet. In 1878 he also became a Justice of the Peace for Buckinghamshire. He continued to live at Rayners and in 1880 is known to have entertained Disraeli, his neighbour from Hughenden Manor and long-standing friend and confidant. In 1881, Queen Victoria also visited, on her way to Hughenden for Disraeli's funeral.

It is known that in 1875 Totteridge House was inhabited by Thomas John Reynolds, as a tenant of Philip Rose. The Rose family continued to own all of their original land in Totteridge, which included the majority of that on the west side of Totteridge Lane almost as far as Terriers. In 1882, Sir Philip extended this by purchasing King's Wood at the auction of the remaining assets of Bassetsbury Manor, and it is reported that the wood was

34   Sir Philip Rose by Spy, in *Vanity Fair*, 1881.

often used for pheasant shoots, to which Sir Philip was very partial. A pair of small houses jointly known as Found Out (sometimes New Found Out), situated at the bottom of King's Wood on the edge of Micklefield, were partially used as Sir Philip's shooting or gamekeeper's lodge, although the houses seem to have existed since the early 19th century or even earlier. The High Wycombe Directory of 1875 records that New Found Out was occupied by James Chapman (keeper) and John Joiner (labourer). It is likely that the dwellings may have been constructed originally in connection with the timber management of the wood. In the 1910 auction notice (see over), the plot was described as consisting of two cottages with offices, sheds that served as a stable, fodder house, cart shed and pig sty, and the cottages occupied by James Roland Fountain and Arthur Wheeler. Later tenants included Mr. Edwards and Wally Soundy. New Found Out with all its buildings was eventually demolished in the mid-1950s.

In 1883, Sir Philip died and was succeeded by his eldest son, Sir Philip Frederick Rose, 2nd Baronet. As the 19th century drew to a close, Totteridge House was still thriving and is reported to have been a fine residence, bustling with servants and activity, and still inhabited by Thomas Reynolds. A clear map of 1898 shows that Totteridge House at this time enjoyed an extensive front garden (now overlaid by the Richard Gardens development), with the main entrance drive extending directly from the front of the house towards Totteridge Lane. Sir Philip and his tenants were clearly enjoying a fine and prosperous life, illustrated by Sir Philip's donation in 1894 of a corner of his main orchard, adjacent to the farm buildings a little further down the lane, for the construction of St Andrew's Mission Church.

At the end of the 1890s the farm was continuing to do well, although the influence of Totteridge House had started to decline, and in the middle years of the decade Totteridge Farm House was constructed to house the farm manager. Nevertheless, in 1910 Sir Philip decided to auction off all his remaining assets in Totteridge. The auction was billed as including 'Totteridge House and Farm, Micklesfield Farm and other freehold properties', and also included King's Wood, New Found Out, Woodman's Cottage and other tracts of land in the area, totalling 13 separate plots. Totteridge House itself, described as an 'Attractive Old-Fashioned Gothic Residence', was listed as possessing a stable, coach-house, harness room and piggeries. The tenant was Mrs. Reynolds, whose husband had died in the early 1900s. The Reynolds family had been the tenants of the house since at least the last quarter of the previous century and continued the Rose tradition of using the venue as one of the main centres of social activity in the village. In the early years of the new century, Mrs. Reynolds continued to host many traditional village events such as the annual fête, and entertained to dinner members of local societies. She was widely known in the area as an exceptionally charitable lady who always enjoyed

35   Front of the auction notice for Totteridge House and Farm, 1910.

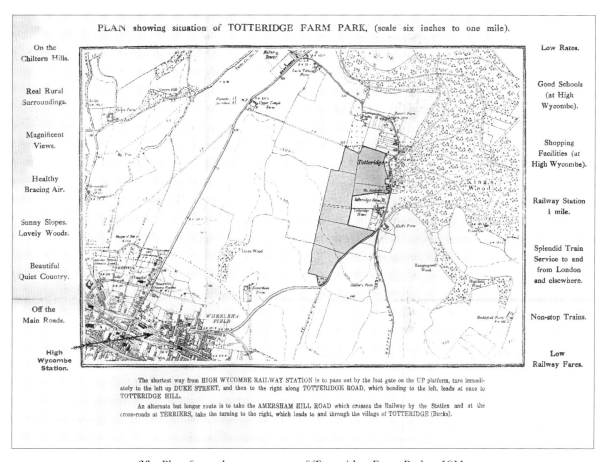

36 Plan from the prospectus of Totteridge Farm Park, *c.*1911.

immersing herself in a wide variety of village occasions. The Reynolds family continued to be the occupiers of the house for at least ten years after the 1910 sale, although whether as tenants or the new owners is not recorded. The Reynolds' fourth son, Leonard, joined up when war broke out in 1914, becoming a captain and distinguishing himself by being awarded the Military Cross in 1916. The family name is remembered in Reynolds Close, on the site of the farm.

At the auction, Totteridge Farm House, farm and most of the land surrounding the house was bought by the Town and County Land Company Ltd. of London. The land covered the area from approximately The Crescent only as far as the *Dolphin* on the west side of Totteridge Lane. Woodman's Cottage was occupied by John Eustace, and Totteridge Farm House and farm by Frederick Smith, the farm being recorded as a plot of 96 acres with a 1½-acre orchard next to the farm house. The main part of King's Wood was bought by Messrs. Edward Wootton Dean, timber merchants, apparently 'for military purposes', whilst three acres were sold to Professor Rose, a relative. The wood remained in the possession of E.W. Dean until 1922, when they sold it to Chepping Wycombe Parish Council. The Town and County Land Company started almost immediately selling off the land it had bought to private purchasers. In the 1911 brochure, the farmland was advertised for sale in freehold plots as 'Totteridge Farm Park', described as affording 'a unique combination of REAL RURAL SURROUNDINGS, with magnificent views, healthy, bracing air and sunny slopes, and ACCESSIBILITY to LONDON (by exceptional train service), as well as excellent local facilities for shopping, schools, etc.'

The Town and County Land Company Ltd. gradually sold off the land for development in the 1920s and '30s as the new housing estates quickly spread from Wycombe across farmland to the borders of Totteridge, so that by the end of the 1930s the house was almost surrounded. The house and land was auctioned again in 1936 but neither vendor nor purchaser is recorded. Totteridge Farm House still stood within its original boundaries, its farming activities having been dramatically reduced following the sale of land. At this time the farm was known locally as Hunt's Farm after the occupants, Joe and Daisy Hunt. A part of the land to the south-west of the house was bought in 1939 by Ernest Turner's Electrical Instruments and has now been developed into Turners Drive and Lyndon Gardens.

The community of Totteridge was expanding quickly. In 1950, King's Wood First School was completed on land sold off by Totteridge Farm House and, later in the 1960s-'70s, the Farm House land was further subdivided to allow for the development of additional private houses along Totteridge Lane overlooking the Common. For several decades in the mid-20th century, Totteridge House was owned by the Rayment family, who built a wing onto the house in 1949. Alan Rayment became a millionaire in the motor industry and once sent a scaled-down car to Buckingham Palace for the young Prince Charles. The thankyou letter from the Palace stated, 'We are having trouble keeping Princess Anne out of it!' When Alan died a widower aged 94 in 1986, the house was sold to a family from Middlesex and shortly afterwards converted into flats, as it remains today.

Another spectral tale surrounds Totteridge House. It had always been rumoured that it was haunted by a lady in brown who was said to cross from the house to the farmyard at dusk. In addition, there was one bedroom that nobody would ever sleep in. Fortunately for the current inhabitants, this apparition seems to have become more reclusive in recent years. Totteridge House today stands as a quiet monument to the heyday of Totteridge. It is difficult to imagine the splendour and prosperous life of the building as it was a mere hundred years ago, virtually obscured as it is now by modern development on almost all sides, its garden rudely curtailed and pitiful. The building itself, though, remains impressive and grand, serving as a symbol of the past glories of Totteridge.

37 Totteridge House today.

The *Dolphin* Public House

Perhaps the best known building in Totteridge, the *Dolphin* public house stands firmly in the centre of the village, relatively untouched by the development excesses of the 20th century. As a public house, it has served the village for well over two hundred years and has seen the area develop from a small agricultural community to the one we know today. There is a high likelihood that the pub started its life with an entirely different name. The first reference to the *Dolphin* is a lone entry in the registers of alehouse keepers of Chepping Wycombe dating to 1760, when Richard Tomsey is recorded as the licensee. However, between 1755 and 1766 Richard Tomsey also held the licence of a public house called the 'Crickett Stick', a name which first appears in 1755, and this suggests that the 'Crickett Stick' and the *Dolphin* were one and the same place. The alehouse continued to be recorded officially as the 'Crickett Stick' when Ann Tomsey took over in 1767, but in 1769 the 'Crickett Stick' disappears from the records and Ann becomes the licensee of the 'Dolphin'.

This change of name is not as mysterious as may first appear. 'The Dolphin' is not an uncommon name for a pub but is unusual in the High Wycombe area. As a connection with the aquatic mammal is unlikely, the name probably relates to a renowned ship (similar to the *Mayflower* in Hazlemere). Several ships have been called the *Dolphin* through the ages but perhaps the most famous one, and one that has close ties with the known history of the building, is that built in 1751. The history of this ship is fascinating and, as it may be the namesake of our beloved public house, it is worth relating briefly the highlights of its illustrious career.

The *Dolphin* was a small frigate of 511 tons that had a complement of 160 men and 24 cannons. Built in 1751, it was commissioned the following year by the Hon. Richard Howe (later Earl Howe, Admiral of the Fleet). Unfortunately, there is no connection with the present Howe family of Penn. The ship started its life relatively quietly, serving its first few years in the Mediterranean and then on patrol around the coasts of England. However, life for the English fleet hotted up in 1756 when the conflict between Britain and France extended to North America as they struggled for dominance over the New World. The *Dolphin* was sent over in 1761 and was engaged in several actions against the French. The conflict ended in 1763 with the expulsion of the French from the Americas, and our ship survived intact with an enhanced reputation. Indeed, one of the French ships captured by the frigate was even renamed *Dolphin's Prize*.

The period following this turned the *Dolphin* into a ship of fame whose name became well known across Britain. In 1764 it was commissioned for an expedition of discovery in the Pacific under captain John Byron. Over two years, several new islands in the South Pacific were discovered and named by

38 Painting of John Byron and his ships *Dolphin* and *Tamar* arriving in Patagonia.

Byron, the ship returning to Britain in 1766 when captain Samuel Wallis took over the helm. Wallis went into the Pacific again, taking a different course to Byron, and opened up a whole new area of the Pacific region, in the Low Archipelago. One of Wallis's most famous discoveries was the island of Tahiti, reached in 1767 and originally named King George the Third's Island, from where Wallis went on to discover and name even more islands in the area. By this time, his voyage of discovery was highly celebrated back home in Britain and the fame of Wallis and the *Dolphin* was assured. They returned to Britain in 1768 and received their deserved glory. In 1770 the *Dolphin* sailed to the East Indies for general duties including trading with the Indians. The ship finally returned to Britain in 1776 and in 1777 it was broken up.

The ship, its captain and crew must have been regarded as national heroes after their return from many years of adventure and exploration across the uncharted and treacherous oceans in the late 1760s. It is not unsurprising therefore that the glorious reputation of the ship was commemorated widely in the names of many public houses, including the *Crickett Stick*, renamed by Ann Tomsey in 1769.

Why was there an alehouse in Totteridge at a time when the village was just a small agricultural community? The mid-18th century saw the Wycombe paper- and chair-making industries beginning to expand and flourish and King's Wood was a major source of wood, primarily supplying Bassetsbury

39 The *Dolphin, c.*1880s.

Manor's own mills. The tavern seems to have been perfectly positioned at the edge of the wood for relieving the labourers of their hard-earned wages after a gruelling day. The knowledge that such a haven existed would have encouraged more workers into the wood, thus guaranteeing the success of both the pub and local industry.

Ann Tomsey was the licensee of the *Dolphin* until 1776, after which there are several gaps in the registers. William Wingrove was the occupant in 1781, then William Fawdrey (1783-4), and then John Graveney (or Graveny) from 1785 to 1815. In 1816 Benjamin Stallwood took over but was replaced in 1825 by his wife, Ester. Throughout the 19th century, the *Dolphin* was tied to Wheeler's Brewery of Wycombe. The Wheeler Brewery started *c*.1812 after Robert Wheeler had entered into a partnership in 1808 with Andrew Biddle, whose family had been brewing in Wycombe since the 1780s. The Wheeler family had the controlling interest in the partnership and took over the brewery entirely following Biddle's death in 1827. The family quickly bought or leased a huge number of pubs which eventually stretched from Thame to Windsor and Hayes (including the *Dolphin*, first licensed to Wheelers in 1832). By the late 19th century, Wheelers was the largest brewer in the area, larger than their Wycombe rival, Lucas, as well as Wethered (Marlow), Weller (Amersham) and Brakspear (Henley). The Wheeler family itself became a very notable and wealthy family throughout the century as prime forces in both the local brewing and banking worlds, with Wheelers elevated to the position of Mayor of Wycombe 22 times between the years 1812 and 1886.

The *Dolphin* was heavily modified in the Victorian period, no doubt as a result of Wheeler investment, and most of what can be seen today is a result of this restoration. In 1841, the census tells us that the publican was still Ester Stallwood, now aged 50, who ran the pub with the help of her son, Solomon (aged 15), and daughter Charlotte (aged 20), and possibly her mother Elizabeth (aged 80). The husband, Benjamin, had disappeared completely by this time. The 1851 census shows that Ester was still the publican and that Charlotte had become a lacemaker by trade, although still living at the pub. Solomon had moved out and become a bricklayer's apprentice in Totteridge, having married Harriet from Medmenham, another lacemaker. By this time, Ester's mother had died. Solomon appears later, in the High Wycombe Directory of 1875, where he is now recorded as a fully-fledged bricklayer in Totteridge, with another Stallwood, Daniel (Solomon's son?), recorded as a farmer in the village.

The Wheeler family continued to own the *Dolphin* throughout the 19th century and there is evidence that the family favoured the Totteridge area. In 1854, Robert and Thomas Wheeler took on the lease on Bunces Farm just up the road (see Chapter 3) and later, in 1904, Robert Wheeler (brewer) moved into St John's House at Terriers.

No details of the development of the *Dolphin* are known for most of the later 19th century.

The Return of Public and Beer Houses with Outdoor Licences, dated 29 September 1872, records that the pub was owned by Wheelers Brewery and occupied by William Putman. Wheelers Brewery closed in 1929 owing to economic pressures and Weller's of Amersham closed the same year. The firm's assets were sold, and the *Dolphin* and its attached orchard to the north were sold off to William Smith, a builder by trade. Within a few years, houses were built over some of the orchard above the pub, with Mr. Smith himself inhabiting a secluded house behind. It is interesting to note that even today there is still a covenant on these houses or their land preventing the sale of alcoholic liquor or mineral water.

Since 1930 the *Dolphin* has changed hands several times and seen several alterations. Stan Webster is remembered fondly as being the landlord who looked after the pub in the 1940s and '50s, assisted by his wife Alice, who died in an electrical accident at a hairdresser's. The former stable house was for some years home to Dolphin Antiques, which moved out *c.*1990, and recent building work conducted by the current owners (brewers Greene King plc) refurbished and extended the west bar to include a new dining area.

Another local ghost story originates from the *Dolphin.* It is reported that over the years a noisy but shy ghost has wandered through the kitchen and back-store areas late at night. Known as William (after he had logged on to a till using that name), he makes himself known by moving objects or pushing them off shelves, or even changing radio frequencies! Although he has not been seen directly, furtive shadowy movements are noticed out of the corners of eyes. He is also known to favour the company of the ladies more, as he seldom makes himself known if men are present! Further down the road at the *Golden Fleece*, another mischievous, although less well reported, ghost is reputed to exist.

The *Dolphin* is continuing to evolve and fortunately remains a successful and popular public house, still providing an invaluable service to the extended community of Totteridge, a service which has been maintained now for well over two centuries.

Old Beams

No history of Totteridge would be complete without mention of Old Beams. Built in the latter half of the 16th century, the property can claim to be not only one of the oldest domestic residences remaining in the High Wycombe area but also one of the most attractive. The house is timber-framed and even today some wattle and daub is present in the

40   Old Beams today.

building, possibly dating back to the original construction. The property
is also Grade II listed.

Old Beams started life as a pair of dwellings called Ivy Cottages which,
given their age and position, may originally have been associated with
Highfield Farm just across the lane. It is known that several outhouses and
barns were attached to the properties in the late 19th century, but
unfortunately no firm history is known prior to this time. The first record
we have dates to the mid-1890s when the owner of Ivy Cottages, Charles

Moxham, bought the field behind the cottages (probably from Sir Philip Rose) and developed a trackway which ran from Totteridge Lane, past the cottages and to the field. The cottages were also at this stage combined into one substantial building. In 1897, the land was sold to William White, a dairyman, who altered the property further, attaching a dairy to the building and using the field behind as pasture for his small herd. White sold up in 1908, and soon after this the name changed to Old Beams.

There were several owners of Old Beams over the next few years, but the only one who left any impression was Thomas Henry Harden. Harden, at one time a member of Chepping Wycombe Parish Council, bought the property in 1917 after he had retired from his profession as a 'Fancy Draper' with premises at 11 High Street, High Wycombe. He also changed the character of the place, closing down the dairy and dividing up the field, adapting one half into an orchard. He died in 1929 and his widow then sold off the field for development, but continued to live in Old Beams until her death in 1939. In honour of her husband, the field was named Hardenwaye. Hardenwaye was a two-acre plot, one half of which was developed in the 1930s in the Old Hardenwaye square we see today, the other half developed as a part of the post-war steel-framed housing estate. Some of the trees still fruiting in the centre of Old Hardenwaye today date back to the time of Harden's original orchard of the 1920s.

The story of Old Beams offers us a limited view of how one small area of Totteridge has adapted and helped to shape the village we know today. The house looks timeless and disguises its 20th-century alterations well, standing steadfastly in a community that has changed almost beyond measure over the four centuries since the original cottages were built.

Totteridge House has illustrated the opulent side of Totteridge village life through the ages, and the *Dolphin* the industrious; Old Beams is the only other building that harks back to the traditional and more tranquil agricultural roots of the village, symbolising the continuity of the past into the present and providing the hope that Totteridge will retain its own independent character for many more centuries to come.

BIBLIOGRAPHY

1841 Census Returns : Wycombe (1841)

Ashford, L.J., *The History of the Borough of High Wycombe—From its Origins to 1880* (1960)

Blair, J., *Anglo-Saxon Oxfordshire* (1994)

Bryant, A., *Map of the County of Buckingham, from an Actual Survey in 1824* (1825)

Bucks. Family History Society, *1851 Census of High Wycombe* (1994)

Bucks. Record Society, *The First Ledger Book of High Wycombe* (1956)

Burke's Peerage Ltd, *Burke's Peerage and Baronetage* (1978)

Clarke, A.A., *Tony's War* (1995)

Collard, M., 'Excavations at Desborough Castle, High Wycombe, 1987', *Records of Buckinghamshire, Vol. 30* (1988)

Colmer, F., 'Archaeological Discovery at Terriers', *Bucks Free Press* (1929)

Colmer, F., 'In Search of a "Castle". Explorations in King's Wood : Prehistoric Totteridge', *Bucks Free Press* (1931)

Dalton, J.N., *The Manuscripts of St George's Chapel, Windsor Castle* (1957)

Dixon, P., *Brewers, Pubs, etc., in High Wycombe 1812-1929* (1985)

Farley, M., 'The Buckinghamshire Chilterns in Later Prehistory', *Chiltern Archaeology—Recent Work* (1995)

Gantzel, D.H., *Hazlemere* (1988)

Gelling, M., *Signposts to the Past* (1978)

Hoing, E., 'E.H. Writes', *St Francis Church—Terriers Parish Magazine* (1978)

King's Wood Conservation Group, *A Walk in King's Wood* (1984)

Mawer, A. and Stenton, F.M., *The Place-names of Buckinghamshire* (1925)

Mayes, L.J., *The History of the Borough of High Wycombe—From 1880 to the Present Day* (1960)

Page, W. (ed.), *Victoria History of the County of Buckinghamshire—Vol. 3* (1925)

Parker, J., *The History and Antiquities of High Wycombe in Buckinghamshire* (1878)

Pevsner, N. and Williamson, E., *The Buildings of England—Buckinghamshire* (1994)

Pike, A., 'Earthwork Enclosures in the Buckinghamshire Chilterns', *Chiltern Archaeology—Recent Work* (1995)

Sheahan, J.J., *The History and Topography of Buckinghamshire* (1861)

Sparkes, I.G., *High Wycombe—A Pictorial History* (1990)

Sparkes, I.G., *The Book of Wycombe* (1979)

Taylor, D., *Terriers House—an Illustrated History* (1984)

Veysey, J., *The On-going Story of a Church* (1995)

Vollans, E.C., *The Evolution of Farm-lands in the Central Chilterns in the Twelfth and Thirteenth Centuries* (1959)

INDEX

References to illustrations are given in **bold**

Aldridge, J., 39
Aldridge, Percy, 34
Amersham, 6
Azor, 1

Ball, Miss A., 39
Barton Lodge, 32, 47, 49, 50, 55
Basset: Alan, 7; Gilbert, 6; Thomas, 6
Bassetsbury Manor House, **11**, 28
Bassetsbury Manor, 7, 9, 10, 14, 15-17, **23**, 28, 60, 61, 72
Beech Tree, 58
Birch, John, 15
bombs, 44-5
Bond, James, 36
Bowerdean, 12, 47, 58
Bowerdean Farm, 32, **35**, 61
Bowerdean Farm Estate, 36, 38
Brakspear's brewery, 72
Brands House, 45
Bridge Mill, 14
Bristow: Frederick, 21; James, 21
Bronze Age, 4
Bryant's map, **2**
Bucks Free Press, 2, 21
Bunce, John, 19
Bunce's Farm, 19, **22**, 22, 38, 72
Byron, John, 68-9, **69**

Carter, Elsie, **51**, 51, 52
Castle Hill, 4, 12
census: 1841, 19-21, 61; 1851, 19-21, 61
chair-making, 11, 14, 15, 21, 28, 31, 58
Chalgrove, Battle of, 4, 13
Chapman, James, 63
Chepping Wycombe Parish Council, 36, 56, 66
Civil War, 3, 13
Clarke, William, 8

Clay, Dick, 47, 49
Clinch, Aubrey, 39, 47
Clissold, Rev. C.H., 34
cock-fighting, 12
Colmer, Francis, 2-3
Colston, Charles, 39
Common Cottages, 17, 58
conservation areas, 58
Coppice Pond, 11, 59
Corporation of High Wycombe, 36
Cotyngham family, 8
Cox, David, 52
Coxham, Charles, 75
Crescent, The, 38, 40, 45, 47, 50, 65
'Crickett Stick', 68, 69

Dashwood family, 14, 28
Dean, Edward Wootton, 36, 66
Desborough Castle, 3
Despenser family, 7
Dolphin Antiques, 73
Dolphin, xi, 2, 3, 15, 19, 20, 21, 24, 36, 39, 45, **46**, 50, 55, 58, 59, 60, 65, 68-73, **69**, **70-1**, 75
Domesday Book, 1, 6
Duchy of Lancaster, 7, 9
Dupont Cottages, 31, 58
Dutton, Edwin, 20
Dutton, Thomas, 19, 20

East Drive, 38
Ecclesiastical Commissioners, 28
Edward II, 7, 8
Edward III, 8
Eldridge, Philip, 50
Elora Road, 35
Ernest Turner's Sports Ground, 41-2, **47**, 57
Eustace, John, 65
Everest Road, 51

Fawdrey, William, 72
First World War, 32, 34
Flackwell Heath, 28
football, 40-1, 42, **44**
Found Out (New), 44, 63
Fountain, James Roland, 63
Four Ashes, 9, 45
Fowler, Charles, 61
Fremantle Road, 50

ghosts, 47-9, 66, 73
Golden Fleece, 51, 73
Gregson, Victor, 34
Grove, Thomas, 15
Gynant's Fee, 6

Hampden: John, 13; Thomas, 8
Harden, Thomas Henry, 75
Hardenwaye, 39, 47
Hardenwaye, Old, 75
Hatters Farm, 15, 34, 45, 51
Hatters Lane, 15, 32, 38, 51, 55, 58
Hatters Lane School, 40, 51
Hazel, James, 21
Hazlemere, 4, 5, 10, 22, 28, 57, 58
Hedge Paper Mill, 14, 17, 28
Henry II, 6,
Henry IV, 7, 9
Hicks Farm, 9, 12, 15, 19, 20, 21, 34, 38, 39, **40**, **49**, 49, 61, 74
Hicks Farm Rise, 50, 58
High Field, 9, 12
Highfield Farm, 12, 15, 19, 38, 45, 47-9, 50
Highworth Combined School, 3, 15, 20, 31, 32, 55, 57, 58
Hill House, 32, 39, 50
Hillary Road, 51, 55
Hollis Road, 52, 53
Holy Trinity Church, 22, 28
Howe, Hon. Richard, 68
Howse, Eileen, 56
Hughenden Valley, 4
Hunt, Joe and Daisy, 66
Hunt Road, 51
Hutchen, Richard, 19

Ingledell, 39, 50
Iron Age, 1, 3-4
Ivy Cottages, 74

John, King, 7, 10
Johnson, Sir Robert, 13
Joiner, John, 63

Keen, Joan, 59
Keep Hill, 28
Kibble: Albert, 45-6; Cath, 45; Len, 45-6; Samual, 34
King's Mead, 14, 28
King's Wood, xi, 2, 3, 6, 10-13, 14, 15, 16, 17, 19, **25**, 28, 31, 32, 36, 39, 44, 45, 51, 55, 57, 59, 61, 63, 65
King's Wood County Junior School, 52-3
King's Wood House, 12
King's Wood Infant School (County First School), 51-3, **52**, **53**, 66
King's Wood Lane, 17, 19
Kingswood Place, 57
Kingswood View, 39

lacemaking, 21
Ladies Mile, 9
Larkfield Close, 58
Line family, 39
Little Totteridge Farm, 12, 15, 19, 20, 21, 22, 45, 49
Little Totteridge House, 3, 32
Loudwater Mill, 14, 17, 28
Lucas' brewery, 72
Lyndon Gardens, 44, 57, 66

Magna Carta, 7
Manor of Wycombe, 6
Marsh Green, 28
Mayo family, 47
Micklefield, 3, 39, 50, 63, **64**
Military College, 16
Mines, Jack, 34
Missenden Abbey, 9
Montfort, Simon de, 9
Moore, George, 34
Mountain Ash Stores, 39

Neolithic period, 4
New Drive, 38, 47
North Drive, 38

Oakridge Farm, 14, 17, 28
Old Beams, 12, 15, 20, 39, 39, 58, 60, 73-5, **74**

Paine, William, 19, 21
paper-making, 14, 15, 21
Peasants Revolt, 8
Penn, 15
Perfect, Stan, 40
Pinions, 14, 45
Pirenore, 5, 9
place-name, 1-2
Plumridge, Mrs. J., 39
Post Office, 17, **26-7**, 31, **34**, 39, 58
Putnam: Amos, 45; Herbert, 34; Ron, 45; William, 24, 73
Putnam's butchers, 39, 55, 59

Quadrant, The, 47

Rayment, Alan, 66
Rayners, 61
Reynolds Close, 61, 65
Reynolds, Leonard, 65
Reynolds, Mrs., 24, 63
Reynolds, Thomas John, 24, 61, 63
Richard Gardens, 58, 63
Richard I, 7
Roman period, 4-5, 6
Rose family, 60, 61
Rose, George, 19, 61
Rose, Sir Philip, 28, 61-3, **62**, 75
Rose, Thomas, 60
Royal Grammar School, 16, 45
Rushbrooke Close, 58
Russell: Caroline, 21; George, 21
Rye, The, 4

St Andrew's Church (Hatters Lane), 55
St Andrews Close, 58
St Andrew's Mission Church, 28, 34, 46, 56-7, **57**, 63
St Francis' Church, 34, 55, 57, 58
St George's Chapel, 9, 10, 13, 14, 28
St John's House, 32, 45, 73
St John's Wood, 28
St Wulfstan's Catholic Church, 53-5
Salter, Miss C., 39, 59
Saxon period, 4-5, 9, 10
Scott family, 47-9
Second World War, 38, 44-6, 55
See of Lincoln, 7
Simmon's farm, 39, **50**
Slater, Constantine, 12, 60

Smith, Frederick, 65
Smith, Tom, 45
Smith, William, 73
Soundy, Wally, 63
South Drive, 38
Stacey, Councillor A., 38
Stallwood family, 19, 21, 72
Stephen, King, 4
Sunday School, 46, 56

Tenzing Drive, 51
Terriers, 3, 4, 5, 9, 12, 14, 19, 20, 21, 28, 32, 36, 38, 45, 46, 50, 58, 61
Terriers First School, **38**, 38, 40, 45, **48**, 52, 58
Terriers House, 58
Terriers Middle School, 55
Tomsey: Ann, 68, 69; Richard, 68
Toterugge, Richard, 8
Toti, 1
Totteridge Arts & Drama Society, 59
Totteridge Avenue, xi, 41
Totteridge Baptist Church, 55
Totteridge Castle, 2-4
Totteridge Common, **ii**, 12, 15, 17, 19, **24**, 28, **31**, 35, 36, 39, 45, 57, 58, 60, 66
Totteridge & District Social Club, 52, 59
Totteridge Drive, xi, 28, 45, 47, 50, 52
Totteridge Farm, 15, 32, 51, 60-7, **64**
Totteridge Farm House, 58
Totteridge Farm Park, **65**, 66
Totteridge Green, 10, 12, 55
Totteridge Hill, 15, 32, **35**, 35, **39**, 39, 45
Totteridge House, 12, 15, 19, 21, **24**, 24, 28, 42, 45, 58, 60-7, **64**, **67**, 75
Totteridge House Cottage, 61
Totteridge Lane, xi, 9, 15, 19, 20, 28, 31, **33**, **34**, 38, **42**, 50, 55, 58, 61, 63, 66
Totteridge Road, xi, 12, 15, **40**
Totteridge Stores, 17
Town & County Land Company, 65
Tucker family, 38
Tuckers Farm, 38
Turner, Ernest, 41, 44, 66
Turners Drive, 44, 66
Tylers Green, 15, 28, 36, 57
Tyzack, Alderman W.H., 40, 50

Tyzack Road, 3, 24, 50, 58

Uplands Close, 38

Veysey, John, 52
Vipont, Ralph, 7

Wallis, Samuel, 68
Webster, Stan, 73
Weller's brewery, 72, 73
West, Rev. James Morgan, 28
West Drive, 38
Wheeler Brewery, 73
Wheeler: Arthur, 63; Robert, 22, 32,
72; Thomas, 22, 72
White Cottage, 17, **20**, 58
White, William, 75
Widmer End, 9
Wingate Avenue, 51
Wingrove, William, 72
Woodman's Cottage, 19, 55, **56**, 63, 65
Wycombe, Chepping and High, 4, 5,
8, 9, 12, 15, 17, 21
Wycombe Hills Squash Club, 44, 57
Wynbury Drive, 39, 55

Young, John, 19, 22
youth club, 56